Best Climbs
Joshua Tree National Park

Best Climbs

Joshua Tree National Park

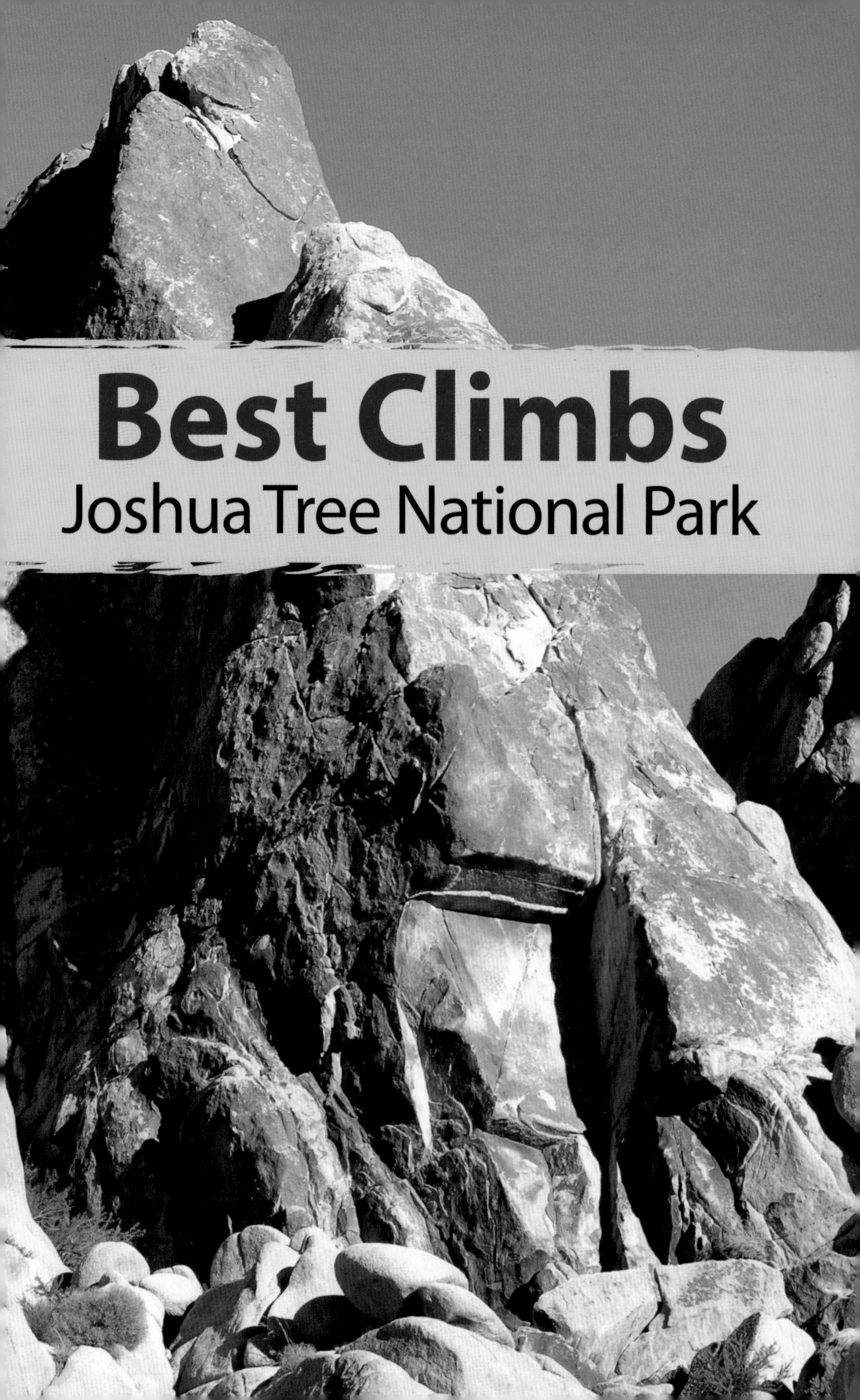

Beth Renn leading *Southwest Corner* (5.6), Headstone Rock.
PHOTO GREG EPPERSON

Best Climbs
Joshua Tree National Park

The Best Sport and Trad Routes in the Park

BOB GAINES

GUILFORD, CONNECTICUT
HELENA, MONTANA

AN IMPRINT OF GLOBE PEQUOT PRESS

To buy books in quantity for corporate use
or incentives, call **(800) 962–0973**
or e-mail **premiums@GlobePequot.com**.

FALCONGUIDES®

FalconGuides is an imprint of Globe Pequot Press.

Falcon, FalconGuides, and Outfit Your Mind are registered trademarks of Morris Book Publishing, LLC.

All interior photos by Bob Gaines unless otherwise noted

Maps and topos by Sue Murray © Morris Book Publishing, LLC

Project editor: David Legere
Text design: Sheryl P. Kober
Layout: Sue Murray

Library of Congress Cataloging-in-Publication data is on file.

ISBN 978-0-7627-7019-9

Printed in China

10 9 8 7 6 5 4 3 2 1

Climbing is a sport where you may be seriously injured or die. Read this before you use this book.

This guidebook is a compilation of unverified information gathered from many different climbers. The author cannot ensure the accuracy of any of the information in this book, including the topos and route descriptions, the difficulty ratings, and the protection ratings. These may be incorrect or misleading, as ratings of climbing difficulty and danger are always subjective and depend on the physical characteristics (for example, height), experience, technical ability, confidence, and physical fitness of the climber who supplied the rating. Additionally, climbers who achieve first ascents sometimes underrate the difficulty or danger of the climbing route. Therefore, be warned that you must exercise your own judgment on where a climbing route goes, its difficulty, and your ability to safely protect yourself from the risks of rock climbing. Examples of some of these risks are: falling due to technical difficulty or due to natural hazards such as holds breaking, falling rock, climbing equipment dropped by other climbers, hazards of weather and lightning, your own equipment failure, and failure or absence of fixed protection.

You should not depend on any information gleaned from this book for your personal safety; your safety depends on your own good judgment, based on experience and a realistic assessment of your climbing ability. If you have any doubt as to your ability to safely climb a route described in this book, do not attempt it.

The following are some ways to make your use of this book safer:

1. Consultation: You should consult with other climbers about the difficulty and danger of a particular climb prior to attempting it. Most local climbers are glad to give advice on routes in their area; we suggest that you contact locals to confirm ratings and safety of particular routes and to obtain first-hand information about a route chosen from this book.

2. Instruction: Most climbing areas have local climbing instructors and guides available. We recommend that you engage an instructor or guide to learn safety techniques and to become familiar with the routes and hazards of the areas described in this book. Even after you are proficient in climbing safely, occasional use of a guide is a safe way to raise your climbing standard and learn advanced techniques.

3. Fixed Protection: Some of the routes in this book may use bolts and pitons that are permanently placed in the rock. Because of variances in the manner of placement, weathering, metal fatigue, the quality of the metal used, and many other factors, these fixed protection pieces should always be considered suspect and should always be backed up by equipment that you place yourself. Never depend on a single piece of fixed protection for your safety, because you never can tell whether it will hold weight. In some cases, fixed protection may have been removed or is now missing. However, climbers should not always add new pieces of protection unless existing protection is faulty. Existing protection can be tested by an experienced climber and its strength determined. Climbers are strongly encouraged not to add bolts and drilled pitons to a route. They need to climb the route in the style of the first ascent party (or better) or choose a route within their ability—a route to which they do not have to add additional fixed anchors.

Be aware of the following specific potential hazards that could arise in using this book:

1. Incorrect Descriptions of Routes: If you climb a route and you have a doubt as to where it goes, you should not continue unless you are sure that you can go that way safely. Route descriptions and topos in this book could be inaccurate or misleading.

2. Incorrect Difficulty Rating: A route might be more difficult than the rating indicates. Do not be lulled into a false sense of security by the difficulty rating.

3. Incorrect Protection Rating: If you climb a route and you are unable to arrange adequate protection from the risk of falling through the use of fixed pitons or bolts and by placing your own protection devices, do not assume that there is adequate protection available higher just because the route protection rating indicates the route does not have an X or an R rating. Every route is potentially an X (a fall may be deadly), due to the inherent hazards of climbing—including, for example, failure or absence of fixed protection, your own equipment's failure, or improper use of climbing equipment.

There are no warranties, whether expressed or implied, that this guidebook is accurate or that the information contained in it is reliable. There are no warranties of fitness for a particular purpose or that this guide is merchantable. Your use of this book indicates your assumption of the risk that it may contain errors and is an acknowledgment of your own sole responsibility for your climbing safety.

Contents

Overview

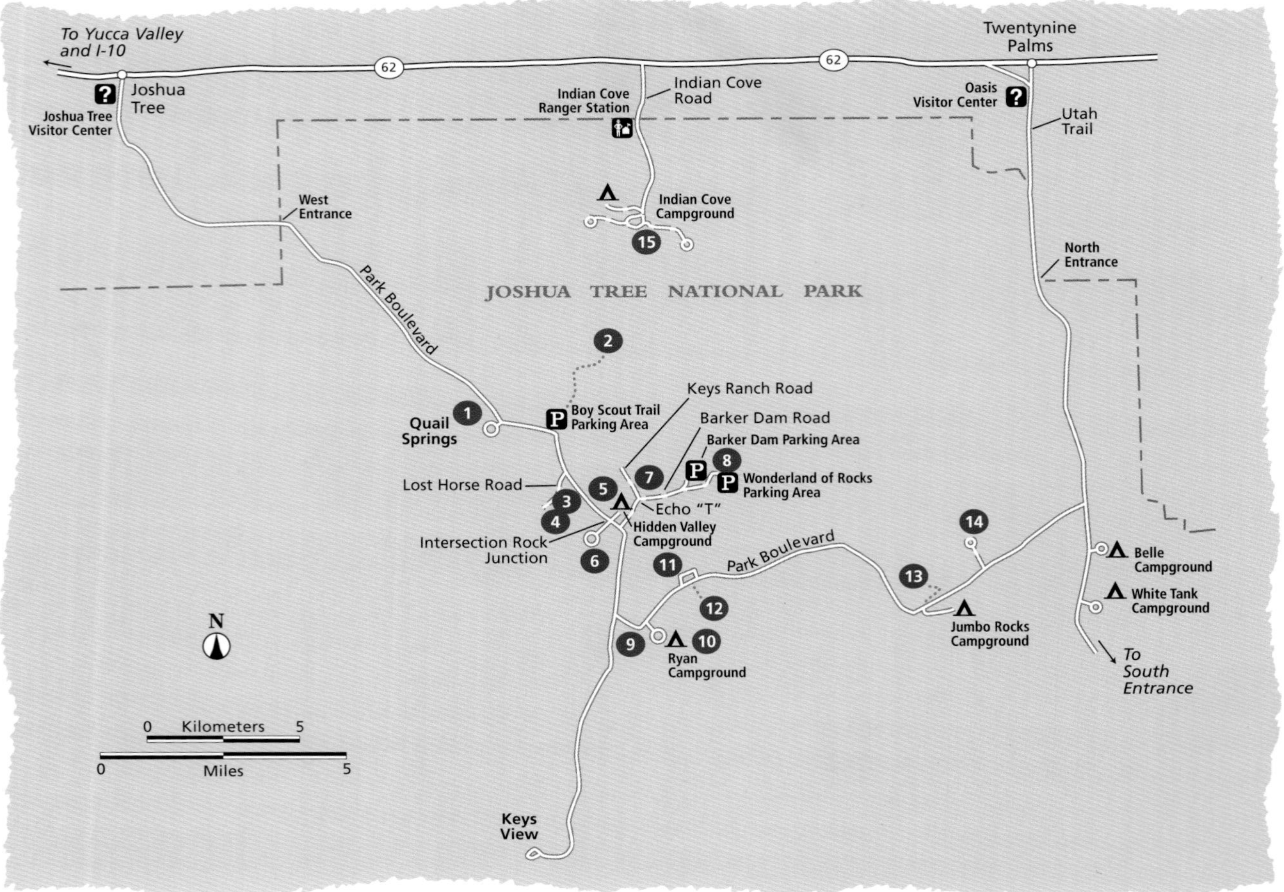

To Yucca Valley and I-10
Joshua Tree
Joshua Tree Visitor Center
62
Indian Cove Ranger Station
Indian Cove Road
Twentynine Palms
Oasis Visitor Center
Utah Trail
West Entrance
Indian Cove Campground
15
North Entrance
Park Boulevard
JOSHUA TREE NATIONAL PARK
2
Keys Ranch Road
Boy Scout Trail Parking Area
1
Quail Springs
Barker Dam Road
Barker Dam Parking Area
8
7
Wonderland of Rocks Parking Area
Lost Horse Road
5
3
4
Echo "T"
Hidden Valley Campground
Intersection Rock Junction
6
11
Park Boulevard
14
13
12
Belle Campground
White Tank Campground
Jumbo Rocks Campground
9
10
Ryan Campground
To South Entrance
N
0 Kilometers 5
0 Miles 5
Keys View

Acknowledgments

I'd like to thank Kevin Powell and Greg Epperson for their great climbing photographs. I'd also like to thank Alan Bartlett and Randy Vogel for paving the way with their excellent series of Joshua Tree guidebooks. Thanks to Joshua Tree Climbing Ranger Bernadette Regan for her input on the Leave No Trace and Park Regulations sections of this book. Thanks to Todd Gordon, Dave Mayville, Tony Grice, Tony Sartin, Erik Kramer-Webb, and Doug Nidiver for fielding all my questions on specific route details. Thanks to my wife, Yvonne, for being my best climbing partner.

Introduction

Joshua Tree National Park is one of the world's most popular climbing areas, offering great variety, easy access, stunning scenery, and more than 8,000 routes. Joshua Tree is the best rock climbing area in the country for favorable weather conditions during the winter months due to its Southern California high desert locale, situated just northeast of Palm Springs.

Most of the climbs are one pitch, but several cliffs offer superb multi-pitch climbing. Virtually every conceivable type of face climbing is found on the rough quartz monzonite granite: low-angle slabs with incredible friction, steep vertical face climbing on patina edges, and overhanging jug pulls. The range of crack climbs is astonishing: finger cracks, hand and fist cracks, off-widths, and chimneys. Many climbers tape up to deal with JTree's notoriously rough rock. Most of the climbing in Joshua Tree is traditional, requiring the leader to place gear for protection and anchors.

The park also has a fair number of mixed routes (bolts with some gear placements) and a small percentage of bona fide sport routes.

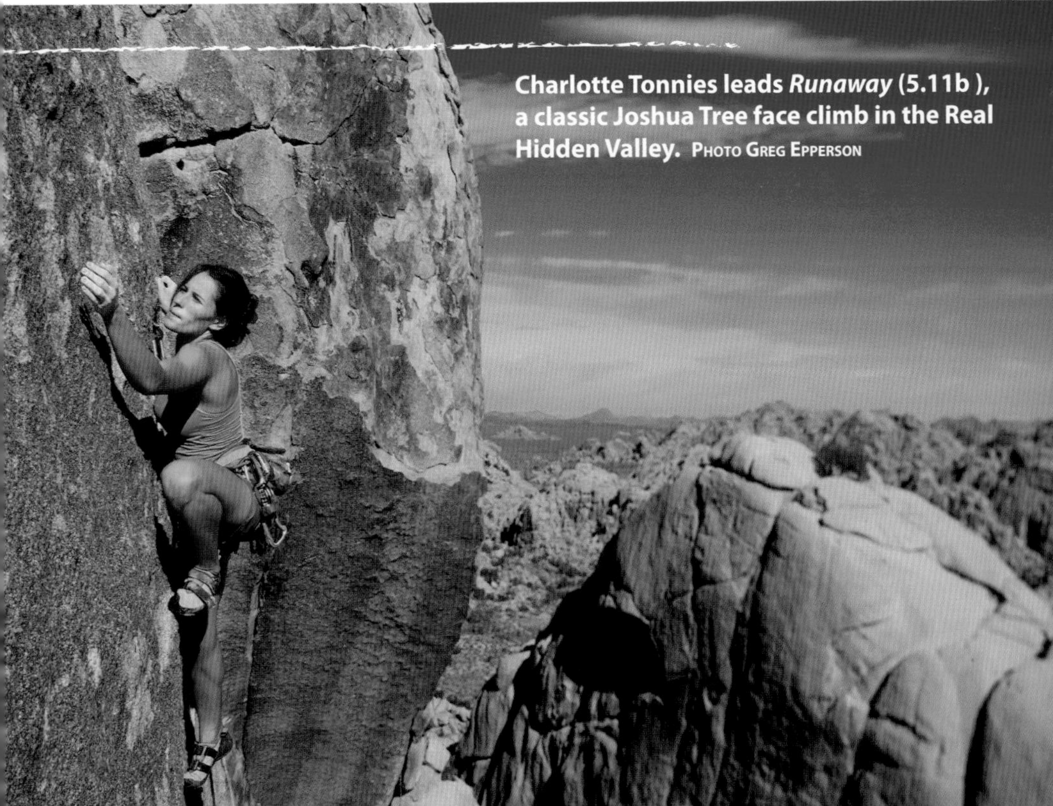

Charlotte Tonnies leads *Runaway* (5.11b), a classic Joshua Tree face climb in the Real Hidden Valley. PHOTO GREG EPPERSON

Joshua Tree National Park

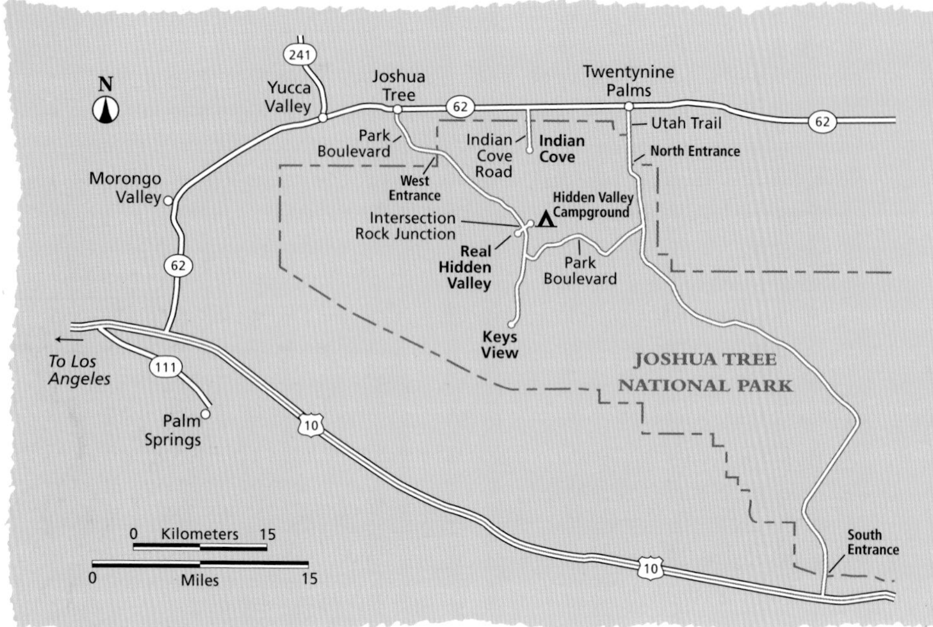

How to Get to Joshua Tree

From Los Angeles: Take I-10 or Highway 60 east to Beaumont/Banning and from there continue east on I-10 past the Palm Springs exit (Highway 111) then take Highway 62 north, then proceed up a steep canyon grade to the town of Morongo Valley. Continue on Highway 62 (now heading east) up another grade to the town of Yucca Valley. A few miles beyond Yucca Valley is the town of Joshua Tree. Turn right on Park Boulevard and proceed 5 miles to the park's West Entrance.

From Orange County: Take Highway 55 north to Highway 91. Take Highway 91 east to Riverside, then take Highway 60 east to Beaumont/Banning where it merges with I-10. Continue east on I-10 past the Palm Springs exit (Highway 111) then take Highway 62 north, then proceed up a steep canyon grade to the town of Morongo Valley. Continue on Highway 62 (now heading east) up another grade to the town of Yucca Valley. A few miles beyond Yucca Valley is the town of Joshua Tree. Turn right on Park Boulevard and proceed 5 miles to the park's West Entrance.

From San Diego: Take I-215/I-15 north to Highway 60, then head east to Beaumont/Banning where it merges with I-10. Continue east on I-10 past the

Palm Springs exit (Highway 111) then take Highway 62 north, then proceed up a steep canyon grade to the town of Morongo Valley. Continue on Highway 62 (now heading east) up another grade to the town of Yucca Valley. A few miles beyond Yucca Valley is the town of Joshua Tree. Turn right on Park Boulevard and proceed 5 miles to the park's West Entrance.

Camping

Campsites at Joshua Tree are beautiful but rustic, with picnic tables and fire rings at each site. A fee is charged for all campgrounds (see the park website for current fees). You must bring your own firewood, as all vegetation in the park is protected. Campfires are allowed only in the fire pits. Each campground has several outhouses. Campsites are limited to six people and two cars per site and are available on a first-come first-served basis, except for Indian Cove and Black Rock Canyon (located just a few miles south of Yucca Valley on Joshua Lane), which can be reserved by calling 800-365-2267 or online at www.recreation.gov. The first-come first-served park campgrounds fill up quickly on weekends during the peak season and holiday weeks. Remember to bring plenty of water; there is no water available inside the park, except for at Black Rock Canyon Campground, which also has flush toilets.

Other Accommodations

Motels and bed and breakfasts are located in the nearby towns of Joshua Tree, Yucca Valley, and Twentynine Palms. Luxury accommodations are available at Palm Springs, about a one-hour drive from the West Entrance.

Supplies and Showers

Climbing equipment is available at Nomad Ventures (760-366-4684, www.nomadventures.com), located on the corner of Park Boulevard and Highway 62 in the town of Joshua Tree.

Camping equipment rentals are available at Joshua Tree Outfitters (888-366-1848, www.joshuatreeoutfitters.com), located 1 block west of the intersection of Highway 62 and Park Boulevard in Joshua Tree.

Showers and supplies are available at Coyote Corner (760-366-9683), located on the corner of Highway 62 and Park Boulevard in Joshua Tree.

The town of Joshua tree has several convenience stores and small markets. Yucca Valley offers a selection of supermarkets including Stater Brothers and Vonns.

How to Use This Book

To select a few hundred "best" routes from 8,000 is no easy task because of what you have to leave out: thousands of good ones and hundreds of great ones. The routes in this book were selected based on rock quality; purity of line (natural lines of weakness up the cliff); fun, interesting, unique, or noteworthy climbing; existing climber access trails; and approaches and descents that do not cause degradation to the fragile desert plant life.

Directions (right or left) are given as if you are facing the route from the base of the route. Directions for climbing, downclimbing, descending, rappelling, etc., are given for the same orientation (as if you were facing the route from the start of the route).

Climbing Instruction

Vertical Adventures Rock Climbing School offers rock climbing classes and guided climbs in the park. Visit www.verticaladventures.com or call (800) 514-8785.

GPS Coordinates

GPS coordinates are given for parking areas, trailheads, key trail turnoffs, and most rock formations. GPS coordinates for rock formations are in most instances taken not at the very base of the cliff, but at key vantage points where you can best survey the routes on the cliff.

Mileages

For climbs in the northwest section of the park, mileages to the parking areas are given from the West Entrance (GPS: N34° 05.612' / W116° 15.900') and also from the intersection of the main park road (Park Boulevard) and the turnoff for the Intersection Rock parking area (referred to as the Intersection Rock Junction, GPS: N34° 00.894' / W116° 09.867'). For climbs in the southeast section, mileages are also given from the North Entrance to the park.

Rappels

Rappel descents are generally less than 30 meters (approximately 100 feet) and can be done with a standard 60-meter rope. Rappels of more than 100 feet require two ropes, or sometimes can be done with a single 70-meter rope where indicated (35 meters, or 113 feet). To prevent rappelling off one or both ends of your rope, or having an accident while lowering, always close your rope system by tying knots in the ends of your rope!

Sport Climbing vs. Trad Climbing

Routes that are entirely bolt protected (with no huge runouts) and have bolt anchors are designated at the start of the route description as "Sport." If a route is not designated as sport, you can assume it's a trad route that requires some if not all gear protection.

Climbing Seasons

Climbing is possible year-round at Joshua Tree, although the prime climbing season is spring and fall. If I had to pick the two best months for reliable, comfortable weather, I'd pick April and October. Early May and late September temperatures average in the 80s and 90s, but temps are often very comfortable in the shade and far fewer climbers vie for the routes than during the peak spring and fall months. The spring (mid-February through April) and fall (October and November) often offer ideal conditions and low probability for storms, and sunny or shady spots can be chosen based on the temps. The door is open, however, for cold fronts to march through Joshua Tree anytime from mid-October through mid-March, and these are often accompanied by Joshua Tree's notorious howling winds, making sheltered, sunny crags the only place to escape the wind-chill factor. Winter (December through mid-February) weather can be spectacular, with cool sunny days, ideal conditions for optimal friction and grip for your best climbs in the sun and on south-facing cliffs. The days are short, however, and if there is a cold front moving through, temperatures can remain in the 40s during the day. During an entire winter season there may be only a few days that receive a light snowfall. Summer (June, July, and August) can be brutally hot, with high temperatures often climbing into the low 100s. Climbing in the summer season is limited to climbing in the shade, very early or very late in the day. There is not much shade to be found anywhere between 11 a.m. and 2 p.m. Occasional cool spells and afternoon thunderstorm clouds can make summer temperatures bearable, but in general it is too hot to climb in the direct sun most of the summer.

Leave No Trace

You can practice Leave No Trace principles from the moment you step out of your car. A few simple steps will help keep Joshua Tree National Park the special place it has been for so long.

- Plan ahead and prepare. Use the outhouses located at most parking areas before you embark on your approach to that day's chosen cliff. Always use the marked climber's access trails where they are available. If there is no marked trail to the cliff, minimize your impact by walking on durable

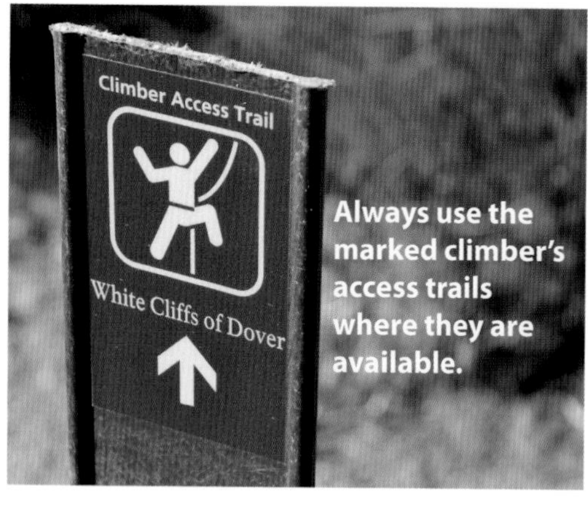

Always use the marked climber's access trails where they are available.

surfaces (e.g., a sandy wash, a rock slab, or barren ground). If nature calls and you're far from any outhouse, deposit solid human waste well away from the base of any climbing site or wash by digging a cathole 4 to 6 inches deep. Cover and disguise the cathole when done. Pack out all toilet paper and tampons in a ziplock bag. Urinate on bare ground or rock, not plants. Urine contains salt and animals will dig into plants to get at it.

- Be courteous of other climbers. Don't make the egregious etiquette violation of monopolizing popular routes by setting up a toprope for a large group. If your climb begins from a campsite, ask permission to climb from the campers if the site is occupied. Minimize your use of chalk, and if you're working a route, clean off any tic marks with a soft brush after you're done.
- Respect wildlife. Pick up all food crumbs and don't feed any of the critters—this habituates them to human food and encourages them to beg and scavenge at campgrounds.
- Leave what you find. All natural and cultural objects are protected by federal law. All historical artifacts (over fifty years old) are protected in the park, as is all vegetation and wood. For more information on helping to preserve the park, contact the Joshua Tree National Park Association at (760) 367-5525 or online at www.joshuatree.org.

Park Regulations

Camping is permitted only in designated campgrounds or with backcountry registration. Off-road driving is prohibited. Park only in designated parking areas, not off the road. Bicycles, including mountain bikes, must stay on established roads.

Dogs must be kept on leash at all times and are prohibited on trails and beyond 100 feet of any campground, road, or picnic area. Please do not bring your dog to any of the climbing areas. Dogs damage vegetation, and their scents are stressful to coyotes, bighorn sheep, and other park animals. For more information on park regulations, visit the park website at www.nps.gov/jotr.

Standard Joshua Tree Rack

A standard Joshua Tree rack includes a set of nuts (stoppers or rocks, perhaps a few medium tricams or hexes) and a double set of camming devices from .4 to 3 inches, plus one 4-inch piece. A few larger cams from 4 to 5 inches are useful for some climbs where indicated. In this book, the size given (e.g., 2-inch cam) refers to the width of the crack, and a camming device with a manufacturer's recommended optimal placement at 2 inches in width will best fit a 2-inch crack. A route description that lists pro as .4 to 1.5 inches means the width of the cracks are .4 to 1.5 inches. A good standard is 6 quickdraws, 6 regular length runners (24 inch), and 2 double length runners (48 inch) along with two 18 to 20 foot cordellettes.

A length of static rope (80 to 100 feet) is very useful to rig topropes on climbs that do not have bolt anchors, which is the standard system used by professional guides. There are many opportunities to utilize huge blocks of rock and situations where the gear placements are located well back from the edge.

A 60-meter rope is the standard climbing rope for Joshua Tree, although a 70-meter rope is useful for rappelling and toproping on some of the taller cliffs.

Many of the climbs have approaches that involve 3rd-class scrambling. Approach shoes with sticky rubber soles are indispensable for Joshua Tree.

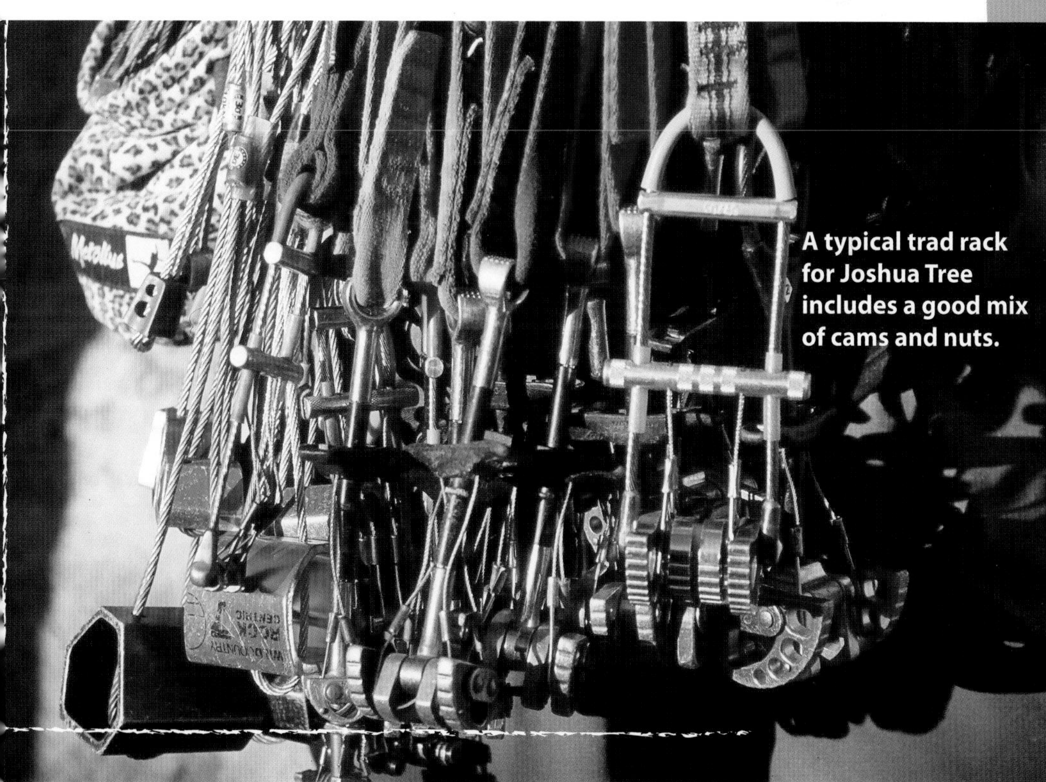

A typical trad rack for Joshua Tree includes a good mix of cams and nuts.

Climbing Safely at Joshua Tree

Safety in rock climbing involves judgment. If you are inexperienced in trad climbing techniques, consider hiring a guide to gain knowledge and confidence. If it's your first time climbing at Joshua Tree, start by climbing below your limit, as techniques for many routes will seem peculiar at first, and ratings will seem underrated until you are more familiar with the rock and its idiosyncrasies. Ratings of PG, R, or X are warnings that the routes have protection problems or include unprotected sections where a fall may result in injury or death. A route rated PG means that there are protection difficulties. The pro may be difficult to place, may require advanced rigging techniques, or may simply be so far below your feet at a crux that you'll be facing a long fall if you come off. An R-rated route designates a route where a fall at the crux will be disastrous, likely resulting in very serious injury or death. An X-rated route designates a complete and utter lack of protection at a crux, where a fall will result in hitting the ground or hitting a ledge and will likely result in death. **Be aware that many routes have easy sections that are rated R or X but are not given that designation in this book.**

If you're leading a route and it doesn't feel right, back off. You may be off-route, on the wrong route, or just having a bad day. Discretion is better than hubris. Many leader fall accidents have occurred when climbers underestimated the difficulty of a climb or their ability to place good protection. *Double Cross,* a 5.8 route on the Old Woman formation, has seen numerous leader fall accidents, even though it has good protection that can be easily placed by a competent leader.

Wearing a helmet is very helpful in preventing head injuries. In numerous climbing accidents involving fatal head injuries, wearing a helmet could have made a difference.

The rock is generally solid, but beware of loose patina plates. Use judgment with detached blocks and boulders when rigging natural anchors at the top of a cliff. Fixed pins should be used with caution and backed up if possible, as they loosen over time due to the extreme hot and cold temperatures.

Most of the routes in this book have had any old bolts replaced. If you do come across a ¼-inch bolt, trust it at your peril, especially if the hanger is rusty or has a bronze tint to it. A few local climbers, led by Kevin Powell, have spent considerable time and effort replacing many of the old bolts in the park with upgraded stainless steel bolts and hangers. The hardware was graciously donated by the American Safe Climbing Association (ASCA). If you'd like to support the ASCA, you can contact them through their website at www.safeclimbing.org.

Joshua Tree has a unique set of objective hazards. Rattlesnakes are rarely seen, but are active in warmer (85 degrees and up) weather conditions. Watch where you step and be aware of your surroundings.

Bees have become more and more prevalent in recent years, and the park is home to both native and hybrid (Africanized) honey bees, which can be very aggressive. Never go near a known hive, and if you're allergic, carry a bee sting kit (epi pen) just in case. If bees start pestering you at a climbing site, it's best to leave the area.

Emergencies

In the event of an emergency, call the park dispatcher at (909) 383-5651 or call 911. Cell phone service is extremely limited in the park and should not be relied upon. Emergency telephones are located at the Intersection Rock parking lot and at the Indian Cove Ranger Station. For minor medical emergencies, the Hi-Desert Medical Center (6601 White Feather Road, 760-366-3711, www.hdmc.org) is located in the town of Joshua Tree. From the intersection of Highway 62 and Park Boulevard, drive 2.2 miles east (toward Twentynine Palms) and turn right on White Feather Road. The emergency room is located 1 block on the left.

Climb Finder

Best Crags for Toproping

Trashcan Rock, Chapter 1
Echo Cove—West End, Northeast Face, Chapter 7
Short Wall, Right Side, Chapter 15
Pixie Rock, Chapter 15

Best Moderate Trad Single Pitch Routes (5.1 to 5.9)

Upper Right Ski Track (5.1), Chapter 5, Intersection Rock
The Bong (5.5), Chapter 5, The Blob
The Eye (5.5), Chapter 5, Cyclops
Double Dogleg (5.7), Chapter 3, Rock Garden Valley
White Lightning (5.7+), Chapter 4, Hemingway Buttress—Main Wall
Sail Away (5.8), Chapter 6, Hidden Tower
Double Cross (5.8), Chapter 5, Old Woman
Dogleg (5.9-), Chapter 5, Old Woman
Cakewalk (5.9), Chapter 3, Freeway Wall
Popular Mechanics (5.9), Chapter 1, White Cliffs of Dover

Best Moderate Trad Multi-pitch Routes (5.6 to 5.9)

Right On (5.6 PG), Chapter 12, Saddle Rock
Mike's Books (5.6), Chapter 5, Intersection Rock
Fote Hog (5.7 PG), Chapter 6, The Sentinel
The Swift (5.7), Chapter 3, Lost Horse Wall
Overhang Bypass (5.7), Chapter 5, Intersection Rock
Mental Physics (5.7), Chapter 8, Lenticular Dome
Walk on the Wild Side (5.8 PG), Chapter 12, Saddle Rock
Direct South Face (5.9), Chapter 15, Moosedog Tower
Dappled Mare to *Roan Way* (5.9-), Chapter 3, Lost Horse Wall
Breakfast of Champions (5.9- PG/R), Chapter 8, South Astro Dome

Best Hard Trad Single Pitch Routes (5.10 to 5.12)

Prepackaged (5.10a), Chapter 4, Hemingway Buttress—Main Wall
Diamond Dogs (5.10a), Chapter 11, Middle Formation
Bird of Fire (5.10a), Chapter 14, Isles in the Sky
Poodles Are People Too (5.10b), Chapter 4, Hemingway Buttress—Main Wall
Taxman (5.10a/b), Chapter 4, IRS Wall
Sidewinder (5.10b PG/R), Chapter 5, Sidewinder Cliff
Illusion Dweller (5.10b), Chapter 6, The Sentinel
Dog Day Afternoon (5.10b PG), Chapter 11, South Rock
Rubicon (5.10c), Chapter 14, Rubicon Formation
The Decompensator of Lhasa (5.10d PG), Chapter 5, Grain Surgery Cliff
Clean and Jerk (5.11a), Chapter 6, Sports Challenge Rock
O'Kelleys Crack (5.11a/b), Chapter 7, Rusty Wall
Jumping Jack Crack (5.11b), Chapter 5, Sidewinder Cliff
Coarse and Buggy (5.11b), Chapter 4, Dihedral Rock
Left Ski Track (5.11b), Chapter 5, Intersection Rock
Hot Rocks (5.11b/c), Chapter 5, Rock Hudson
Wangerbanger (5.11c), Chapter 7, Rusty Wall
Spider Line (5.11d), Chapter 5, Old Woman
Campfire Girl (5.12a), Chapter 15, Campfire Crag
Leave It to Beaver (5.12a), Chapter 6, Sports Challenge Rock

Best Hard Trad Multi-pitch Routes (5.10 to 5.11)

Bird on a Wire (5.10a), Chapter 3, Lost Horse Wall
Ball Bearing (5.10a), Chapter 6, The Sentinel
Santa Cruz (5.10a), Chapter 11, Saddle Rock
My Laundry (5.10a), Chapter 8, South Astro Dome

Solid Gold (5.10b PG), Chapter 8, South Astro Dome
Figures on a Landscape (5.10b PG), Chapter 8, North Astro Dome
Where Have all the Cowboys Gone (5.10d), Chapter 11, Saddle Rock
Such a Savage (with direct start) (5.11a), Chapter 8, South Astro Dome
Astroturf (5.11a R), Chapter 8, North Astro Dome
Swept Away (5.11a), Chapter 7, Echo Rock—South Face

Best Sport Climbs

Swing Low (5.7+/5.8-), Chapter 7, Echo Cove—West End
Binder (with *Crossroads* finish) (5.8), Chapter 2, Eastern Siberia Cliff
Incandescent (5.8), Chapter 7, Little Hunk—Northeast Face
Cryptic (5.8), Chapter 10, Headstone Rock
Sexy Grandma (5.9-), Chapter 5, Old Woman
Yasmine Bleath (5.10a), Chapter 2, Eastern Siberia Cliff
Dos Chi Chis (5.10a), Chapter 2, Eastern Siberia Cliff
Toby (5.10a), Chapter 2, Eastern Siberia Cliff
Peewee's Piton (5.10a) Chapter 5, Peewee Rock
The Paw (5.10c), Chapter 7, Little Hunk—Southeast Face
Blues Traveler (5.10c/d), Chapter 7, Little Hunk—Northeast Face
Pet or Meat (5.10d), Chapter 15, Feudal Wall
Physical Graffiti (5.11a), Chapter 7, Anasazi Wall
Blackjack (5.11a) Chapter 4, Ken Black Memorial Dome
Boulderado (5.11a), Chapter 13, Conan's Corridor
Runaway (5.11b) Chapter 6, Tumbling Rainbow Formation
Jane's Addiction (5.11b), Chapter 11, North Rock
Changes (5.11c/d) Chapter 7, Little Hunk—Northeast Face
Electric Blue (5.11d) Chapter 7, Little Hunk—Northeast Face
Rap Bolters are Weak (5.12a), Chapter 6, Sports Challenge Rock
Cutting Edge (5.13b), Chapter 10, Headstone Rock

Best Face Climbs (Mixed Trad and Sport)

Southwest Corner (5.6), Chapter 10, Headstone Rock
Stichter Quits (5.8), Chapter 7, Echo Rock—Main Slab
Dazed and Confused (5.9 PG), Chapter 8, Lenticular Dome
Rock Candy (5.9+ PG), Chapter 3, Rock Garden Valley
ZZZZ (5.9+ PG), Chapter 7, Little Hunk—Northeast Face
Loose Lady (5.10a PG), Chapter 7, Houser Buttress
Run For Your Life (5.10b PG), Chapter 6, Tumbling Rainbow Formation
Space Mountain (5.10b), Chapter 12, Saddle Rock

Sig Alert (5.10c), Chapter 3, Freeway Wall
Harley Queen (5.10d), Chapter 12, Saddle Rock
The Official Route of the 1984 Olympics (5.10d), Chapter 5, Cyclops
EBGBs (5.10d), Chapter 7, Echo Rock—EBGBs Block
Alf's Arête (5.11a PG), Chapter 4, IRS Wall
Good Housekeeping (5.11b), Chapter 1, White Cliffs of Dover
Big Moe (5.11a/b R/X), Chapter 7, Echo Cove—West End
Ground Up or Shut Up (5.11b), Chapter 7, Echo Cove—West End
Rap Bolters Are Weak (5.12a), Chapter 6, Sports Challenge Rock

Map Legend

Symbol	Feature	Symbol	Feature
70	Interstate		Wash
25	US Highway		Mountain Peak
74	State Highway	P	Parking
170	County Road		Restroom
	Gravel or Dirt Road		Building
	Unimproved Road		Camping
	Trail		Gate
	Town		Trailhead
	City		Ranger Station
	Rock Formation		Picnic Area
	Cliff Edge	?	Visitor Center

Topo Legend

o	Belay stance with gear anchor
P	Fixed piton
X	Single piece of fixed protection (bolt or piton)
XX	Fixed belay station

Quail Springs

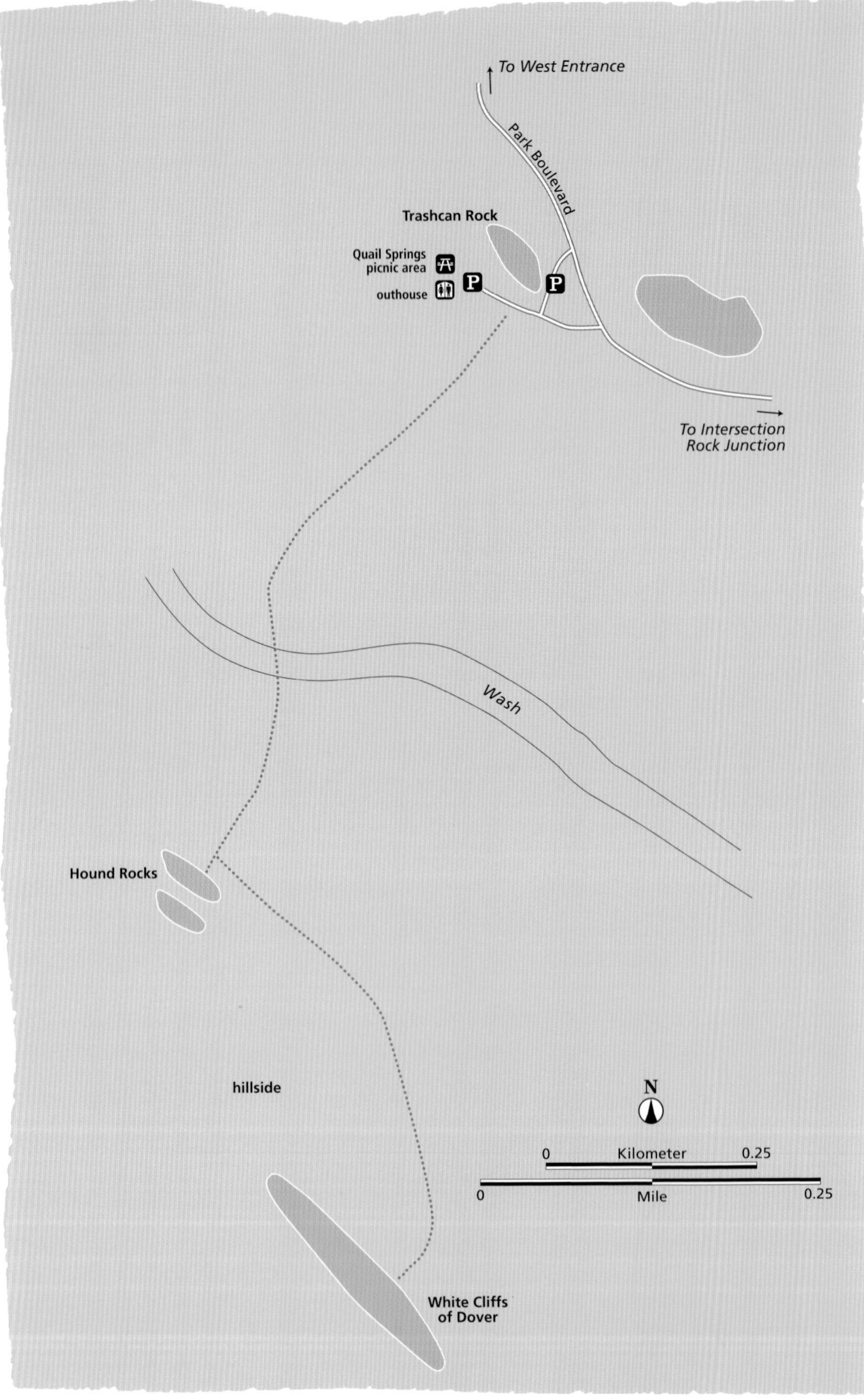

To West Entrance
Park Boulevard
Trashcan Rock
Quail Springs
picnic area
outhouse
P
P
To Intersection
Rock Junction
Wash
Hound Rocks
hillside
N
0
Kilometer
0.25
0
Mile
0.25
White Cliffs
of Dover

1.

Quail Springs

Trashcan Rock at the Quail Springs Picnic Area is one of Joshua Tree's quintessential "roadside crags." A short hike leads to Hound Rocks and two classic 5.10 crack climbs. Farther down the trail, sitting high on a hillside, is the White Cliffs of Dover, featuring Yosemite-like dihedrals and cracks plus a couple of excellent face climbs, all on very smooth, high-quality granite.

Getting there: Drive 5.7 miles from the West Entrance and turn right at Quail Springs Picnic Area. From the Intersection Rock Junction, drive north 2.8 miles and turn left. Here you'll find Trashcan Rock. There is ample parking on the south and west sides of the rock, as well as picnic tables and an outhouse. The trail to Hound Rocks and the White Cliffs of Dover begins at the south end of the parking lot (GPS: N34° 02.388' / W116° 11.835').

TRASHCAN ROCK

Often crowded, especially on weekends, Trashcan Rock is one of Joshua Tree's most popular crags. The routes aren't classics, but the crag is. The west face has a great assortment of climbs for beginners, and the east face has several excellent harder routes. The east face receives morning sun and afternoon shade, and the west face receives early morning shade, then sun all day. **Note:** There are no fixed anchors or rappel anchors on top—all the climbs require gear anchors. Crag GPS: N34° 02.429' / W116° 11.797'

Descent: The easiest approach to and descent from the top is a 4th-class scramble up the northwest side (the far left side of the west face).

Trashcan Rock—East Face

Trashcan Rock—East Face

1. Filch (5.6) Begin off a boulder. Climb the wide crack to thinner jamming.

2. Ripper (5.11a) Crank the overhang to a lieback/jam. Often done as a boulder problem (V2), downclimbing *Filch*.

3. Wallaby Crack (5.9) Jam an awkward flare to the top.

4. Hermanutic (5.10c R) Climb the face and thin crack to a tricky crux with poor pro.

5. Butterfly Crack (5.11c) Jam the classic fingertip crack, with a very hard start.

6. Left Sawdust Crack (5.10c PG/R) Climb the left crack, avoiding the one on the right. Using both cracks at the top makes the route significantly easier.

7. Right Sawdust Crack (5.9) Solid hand jams lead to the top.

Trashcan Rock—West Face

Trashcan Rock—West Face

1. Karpwitz (5.6) Face climb up to a well-protected thin crack crux.

2. B3 (5.3) Smear and jam up the groove.

3. Profundity (5.10b) Friction climb and mantle past two bolts. Reachy.

4. B2 (5.3) Smear and jam up the groove. It's 5.9 if you climb the slab just left of the crack.

5. Tiptoe (5.7) This little gem has you edging and smearing up a thin dike past three bolts. The easiest way to get to the first bolt is by starting up *B2,* then stepping right to the first bolt. Some large camming devices (#4 camalots) are handy to set up a toprope.

6. B1 (5.1) Ascend a groove that leads to a nice combination of face climbing and jamming.

7. Walkway (5.5 R) Make delicate friction moves to an easy jam crack. A 5.6 lieback start can be done just to the right.

8. Baby Point Five (5.10a R) No pro, but a good toprope. A thin move on polished holds leads to easier friction.

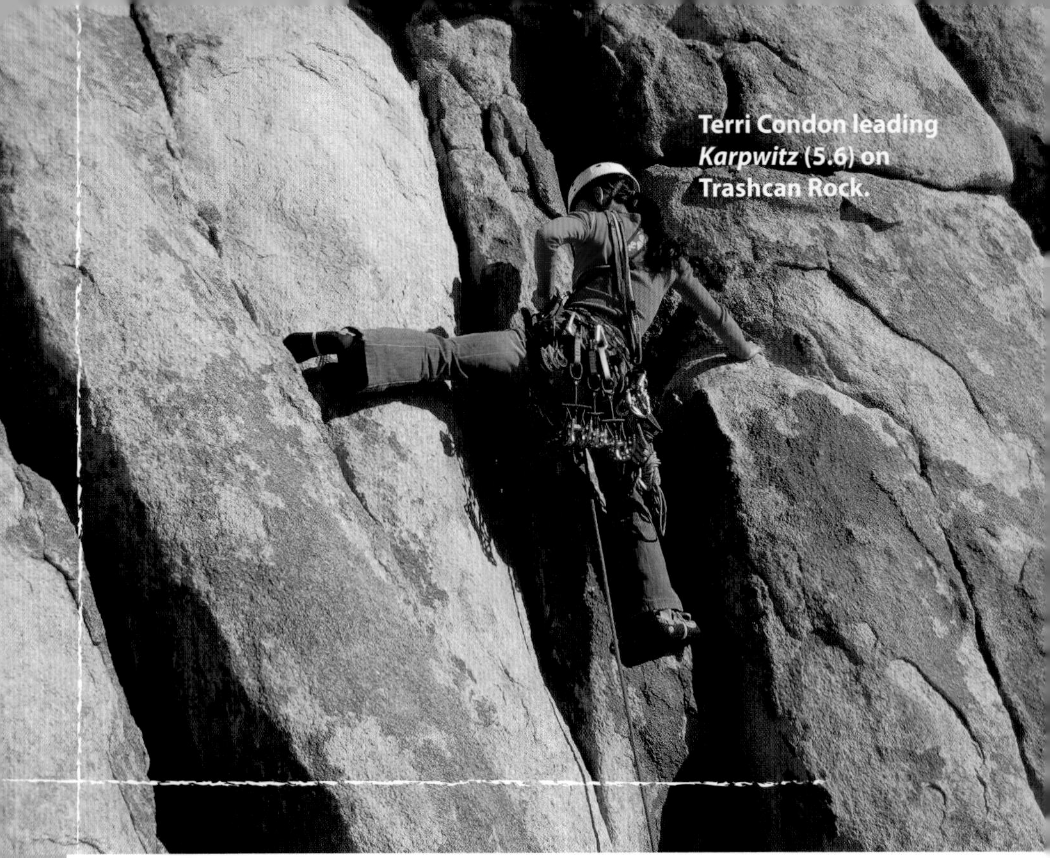
Terri Condon leading *Karpwitz* (5.6) on Trashcan Rock.

9. Tulip (5.6 R) Jam a short groove and finger crack, then smear your way up the slab. One bolt provides rather inadequate protection.

10. Bimbo (5.10a R) Lieback a flake to a seam, then make some very delicate friction moves (crux) to easier smearing.

11. Eschar (5.6) Mantle up to the big ledge, then face climb up to the left-slanting jam crack.

12. Cranny (5.8) Mantle up to the big ledge, then climb a steep wall with two vertical cracks. Nice stemming on the upper section.

13. Bloodymir (5.9) From the big ledge, climb the face on the right past a bolt, then jam the left-slanting crack.

Hound Rocks

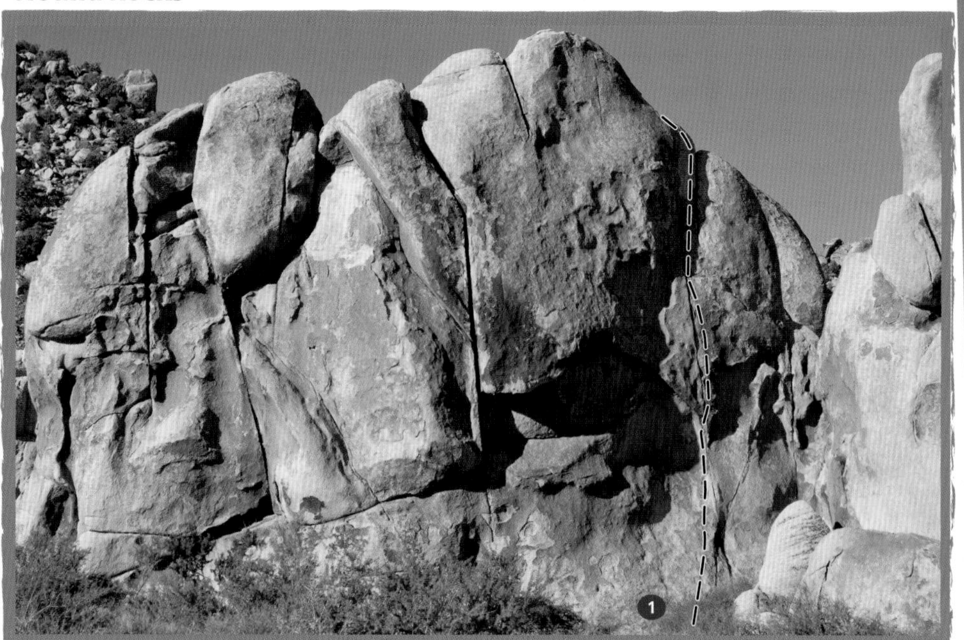

HOUND ROCKS

Hound Rocks consist of two rock formations split by a narrow canyon once used as a miner's camp.

Finding the crags: The trail begins at the south end of the Quail Springs parking lot. Walk west for a few hundred yards to where the trail climbs gently over a sand dune, then drops down and slightly left, crossing a broad, sandy wash. After another few hundred yards, the trail leads directly to the Hound Rocks. The *Right Baskerville Crack* is on the first cliff you come to. *Tossed Green* is on the next formation to the west, accessed by walking around the left side of the first cliff. Both of these climbs face east and receive morning sun and afternoon shade. Crag GPS: N34° 02.028' / W116° 12.089'

1. Right Baskerville Crack (5.10b) Start up a delicate slab, then jam and lieback the steep, thin crack. Route GPS: N34° 02.028' / W116° 12.089'. **Descent:** Downclimb (4th class) off the opposite (west) side of the formation. **Pro:** Some large cams are useful for the anchor.

Hound Rocks

2. Tossed Green (5.10a) Climb the steep finger crack to a 2-bolt belay/ rappel anchor. Route GPS: N34° 02.011' / W116° 12.104'. **Descent:** Rappel from the bolt anchor. **Pro:** Take a good selection of cams from .5 to 2.5 inches.

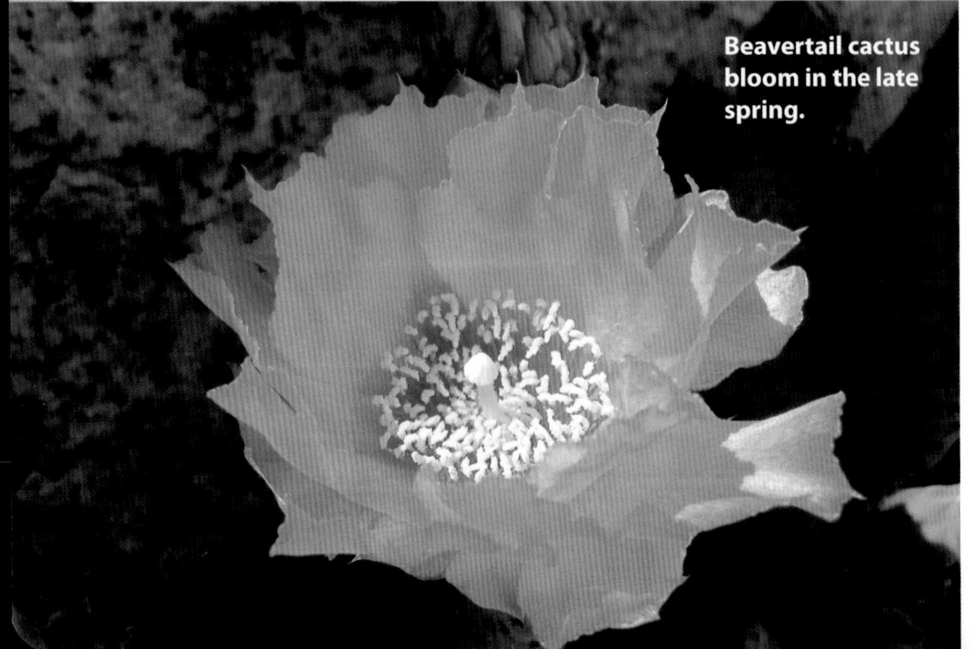

Beavertail cactus bloom in the late spring.

White Cliffs of Dover Overview

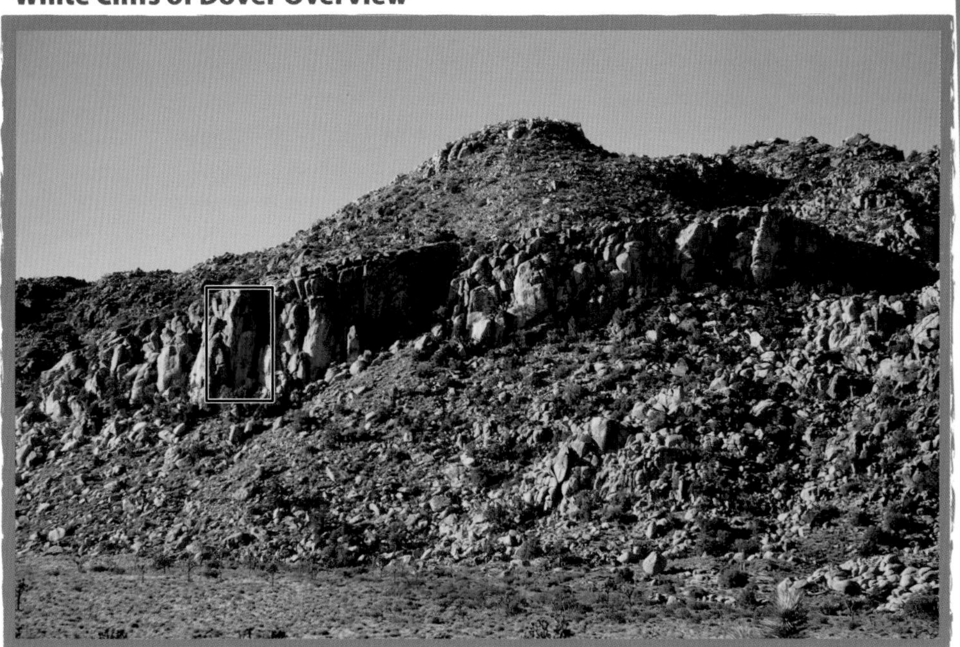

WHITE CLIFFS OF DOVER

These cliffs feature Yosemite-like cracks and corners, along with some stellar face climbs, all on very smooth, fine-grained granite. The east-facing cliffs receive early morning sun, then shade for the rest of the day. In the winter this cliff gets very little sun.

Finding the crag: The trail begins at the south end of the Quail Springs parking lot. Walk west for a few hundred yards to where the trail climbs gently over a sand dune, then drops down and slightly left, crossing a broad, sandy wash. After another few hundred yards, the trail leads directly to the Hound Rocks. Head left and follow the trail as it parallels the base of the hillside to your right for several hundred yards, until it merges into the base of a steeper hillside. From here the trail climbs directly up the hillside to the base of the routes. Approach time is about twenty-five minutes. Crag GPS: N34° 01.820′ / W116° 11.950′

1. Scientific Americans (5.8 PG/R) Begin at the base of *Popular Mechanics* and climb up to a pillar left of a chimney. Clip a bolt, make an extended reach out left, then face climb up to a horizontal crack. Climb past another bolt on the arête/face of the pillar, then follow a crack system and flakes up to the 2-bolt anchor shared with *Ace of Spades.* **Descent:** Rappel 100 feet from the bolt anchor shared with *Ace of Spades.* **Pro:** thin to 2 inches.

2. Ace of Spades (5.9) Climb through the crux of *Popular Mechanics,* then climb double cracks on the steep left wall up to a bolt anchor. **Descent:** Rappel 100 feet from the bolt anchor.

3. Popular Mechanics (5.9) Jam, stem, and lieback up the spectacular corner. The crux is about 15 feet up. **Descent:** Rappel 85 feet from the bolt anchor. **Pro:** medium nuts, cams to 3 inches; bolt anchor.

4. Good Housekeeping (5.11b) Begin 20 feet right of *Popular Mechanics.* Crank steep face moves past a bolt (5.10d) up to a crack (2-inch pro here), traverse left across a thin seam, then climb thin slab moves (5.11b) past a second bolt. At the third bolt move left to the arête, then smear and slap your way up the rounded arête past two more bolts (5.11b) up to a sloping ledge. Gear anchor (1.5 to 3 inches). **Descent:** Belay down to the rappel bolts on *Popular Mechanics* and rappel 85 feet.

White Cliffs of Dover

2. Mongolia

Mongolia is a complex series of ramparts and cliffs located within Joshua Tree's wilderness boundary. If you're looking for moderate, multi-pitch, bolted face climbs on a sunny, south-facing wall, Mongolia's Eastern Siberia cliff is your crag. The routes range from 5.8 to 5.10 and up to three pitches in length. Bring a dozen quick-draws, some slings, and a light rack up to 2 inches. Be prepared to share the crag with others, particularly on weekends. This is a good place to climb during cooler weather. It is sheltered from north winds and gets a lot of sunshine. The area bakes in the sun during warmer conditions. If you climb here, please practice Leave No Trace wilderness ethics, and stay on climber's trails to minimize your impact.

Finding the crag: From the West Entrance, drive 6.4 miles south on Park Boulevard and turn left into

Mongolia

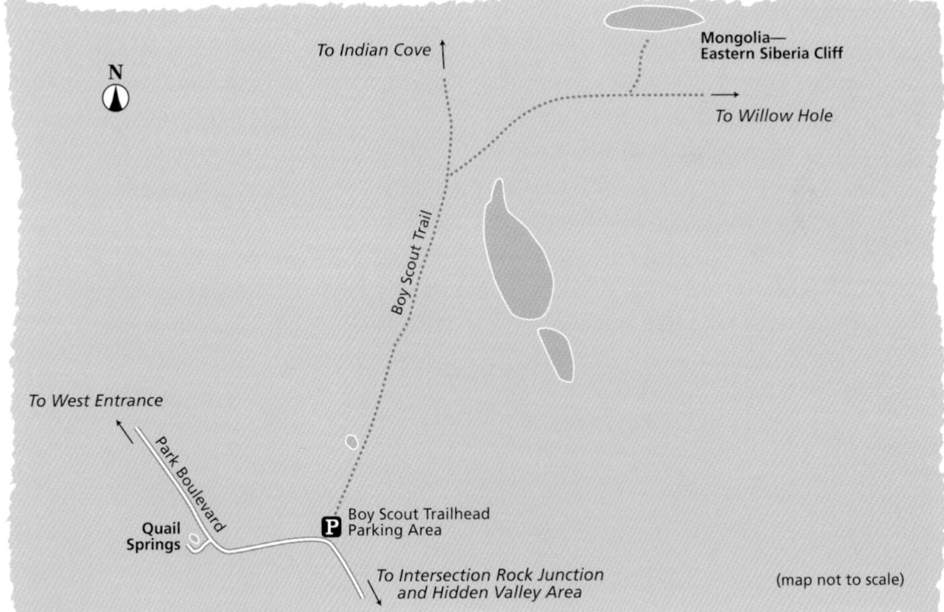

Mongolia Overview

the Boy Scout Trail parking lot. From the Intersection Rock Junction, go 2.2 miles north and turn right. Hike 1.2 miles along the Boy Scout Trail to where it forks, then take the right fork (the Willow Hole Trail) for about 0.75 mile. Turn left off the Willow Hole Trail onto a marked climber's trail (signed Outer Mongolia, GPS N34° 03.938' / W116° 10.310') and follow it to the base of the cliffs (marked Eastern Siberia). Scramble (3rd class) through a boulder-filled canyon, then turn right and follow the base of the main cliff about 200 feet to the right. Approach time is about one hour. Crag GPS: N34° 02.449' / W116° 11.153'

Descent: All of the routes have bolted rappel anchors and can be rappelled with one 60-meter rope, although a 70-meter rope (or two ropes) is handy for rappelling *Bull with Gas/Love Gas/Hollywood Rattlesnake.*

Eastern Siberia Cliff

EASTERN SIBERIA CLIFF

Eastern Siberia Cliff—Left Side

Routes 1 through 3 share the same first-pitch anchor. Crag GPS: N34° 04.193' / W116° 10.183'

Descent: From the pitch 1 anchor, rappel 100 feet with a 60-meter rope plus some downclimbing, or better yet, rappel with a 70-meter rope (or two ropes). From the top of pitch 2 on *Love Gas,* you can rap to the ground with two ropes (less than 200 feet) or make a 100-foot rappel down to the pitch 1 anchor. Beware of knocking off loose plates when rapping down.

1. Bull with Gas (5.9) Start with a low-angle ramp, then move up a steep wall on slightly loose patina plates up and right past seven bolts and a fixed pin to a bolt belay (shared with *Love Gas* and *Hollywood Rattlesnake*). **Pro:** to 2 inches for the ramp at the start.

2. Love Gas (5.10a) **Pitch 1:** Climb the steep face on slightly loose patina plates just right of *Bull with Gas* past six bolts and two fixed pins up to the 2-bolt anchor. **Pitch 2:** Climb the friction slab (5.10a) past two bolts up to a 2-bolt anchor. **Pro:** to 2 inches for the ramp at the start.

3. Hollywood Rattlesnake (5.10a) Begin just right of *Love Gas* and climb straight up past two bolts to a crack (2- to 2.5-inch cam), then angle left up the slab past six more bolts to the bolt anchor. 8 bolts to a 2-bolt belay/rappel anchor. **Pro:** a few 2- to 2.5-inch cams.

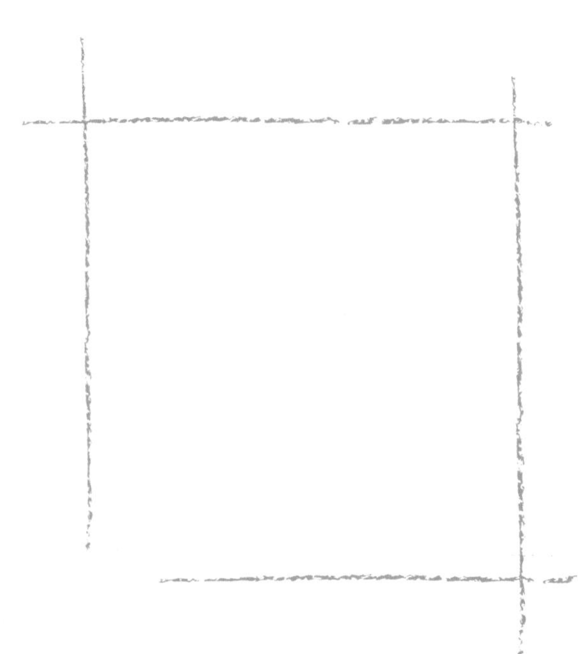

Eastern Siberia Cliff—Left Side

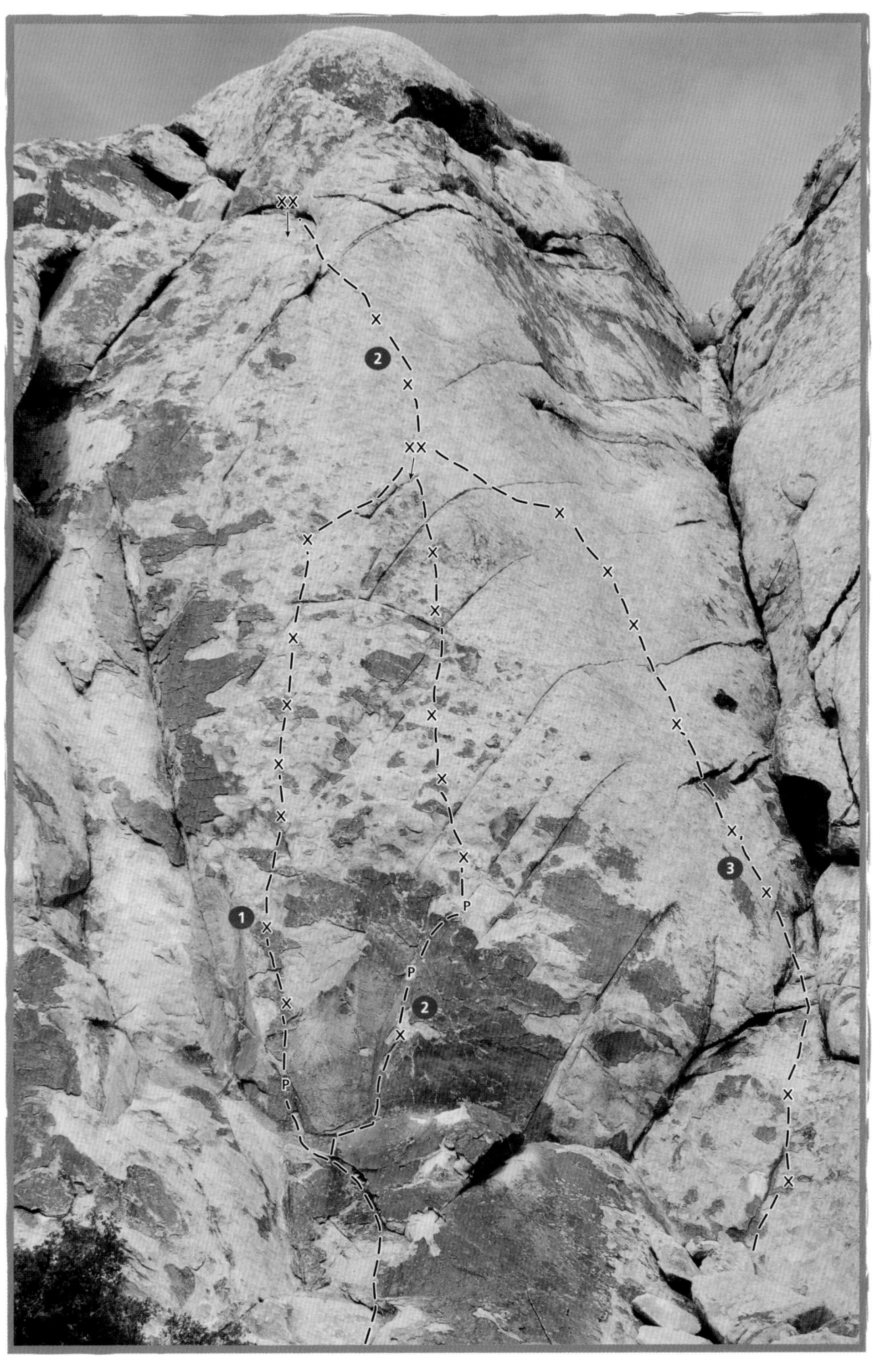

Eastern Siberia Cliff—Right Side

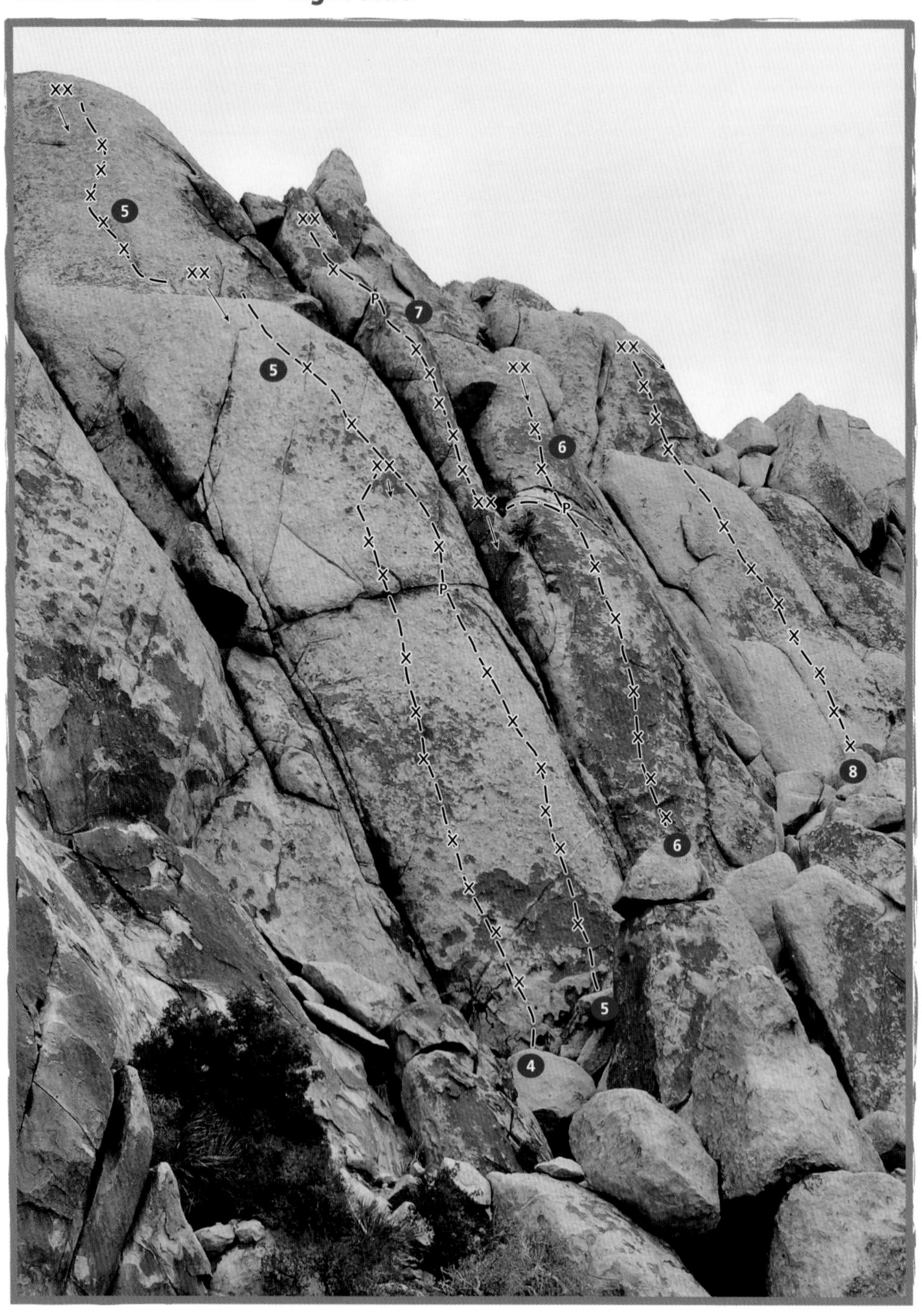

Eastern Siberia Cliff—Right Side

4. Yasmine Bleath (5.10a) Sport. The leftmost route on the central pillar. The start is a little easier by climbing from the right to reach the first bolt. Climb the face past nine bolts to the 2-bolt anchor shared with *Dos Chi Chis.* Rappel from here (less than 100 feet) or continue on *Dos Chi Chis.*

5. Dos Chi Chis (5.10a) Sport. The rightmost of two bolted routes on the central pillar and the best route on the cliff. **Pitch 1:** Climb the wonderfully featured face (5.9+/10-) past seven bolts and one fixed pin to an intermediate anchor (doubled for a rappelling), then up past two more bolts to a huge ledge with a 2-bolt anchor. (Two 100-foot rappels to descend from here.) **Pitch 2:** From the left side of the ledge, climb a delicate slab/arête past five bolts on fairly sustained smearing (5.10-) up to a 2-bolt anchor. From the summit there is a commanding view of the northern portion of the park. **Descent:** Make three 100-foot rappels down the route.

6. Binder (5.8) Sport. Excellent moderate face climbing on the right-hand pillar. Eight bolts and one fixed pin up to a 2-bolt belay/rappel anchor (100 feet).

The Eastern Siberia routes represent the vision and hard work of longtime new-route pioneer and local Todd Gordon, who hand-drilled the bolts on the lead, in the traditional, ground-up style.

7. Crossroads finish (5.7) Sport. Can be combined with *Binder* for a great two-pitch excursion. **Pitch 1:** A good strategy to protect your second is to climb *Binder* (5.8) to the anchor, then lower down to the *Crossroads* anchor about 30 feet down and left and belay. When your second follows, lower them down from the anchor to your belay (you can retrieve your gear on the rappel descent). **Pitch 2:** Fun climbing (5.7) up the face/ arête past six bolts and one fixed pin to a 2-bolt belay/rappel anchor. **Descent:** Make two 100-foot rappels.

8. Toby (5.10a) Sport. Climb the face of a pillar past seven bolts to a ledge, then up past three more bolts to a 2-bolt belay/rappel anchor (100 feet).

Lost Horse Road

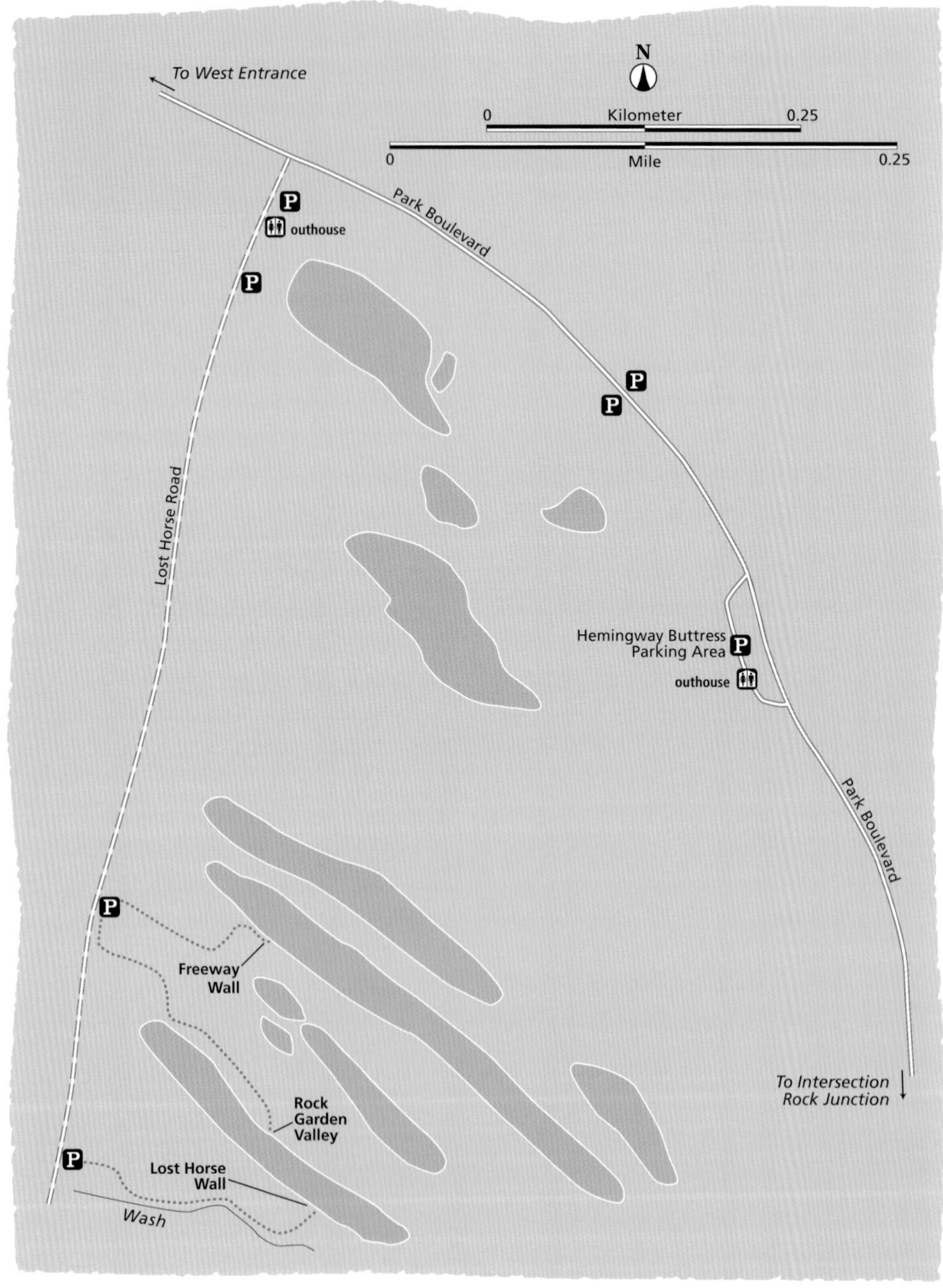

To West Entrance
N
0
Kilometer
0.25
0
Mile
0.25
Park Boulevard
P
outhouse
P
P
P
Lost Horse Road
Hemingway Buttress
Parking Area
outhouse
Park Boulevard
P
Freeway
Wall
Rock
Garden
Valley
P
Lost Horse
Wall
Wash
To Intersection
Rock Junction

3.

Lost Horse Road

This area features a great assortment of both crack and face climbs on excellent, featured rock. The Freeway Wall has some excellent moderate crack pitches, and Rock Garden Valley boasts some classic 5.7 to 5.9 face and crack routes. The 400-foot-high Lost Horse Wall has perhaps the finest collection of moderate multi-pitch trad routes in all of Joshua Tree National Park.

Getting there: From the West Entrance, drive 7.3 miles south on Park Boulevard and turn right onto dirt Lost Horse Road. From the Intersection Rock Junction, drive north 1.3 miles and turn left. Follow directions below for the individual cliffs.

FREEWAY WALL

This tall cliff sits high in a beautiful rocky canyon. It gets shade in the morning, then sun in the afternoon.

Finding the crag: From the intersection of Park Boulevard and Lost Horse Road, drive 0.3 mile down Lost Horse Road and park on the left (GPS: N34° 01.439' / W116° 10.833'). Follow a trail for several hundred feet to a small man-made dam, then head left and scramble up the hillside through the boulders, staying left as you approach the wall. Hiking time is about ten minutes. Crag GPS: N34° 01.390' / W116° 10.709'

Freeway Wall/Rock Garden Valley Overview

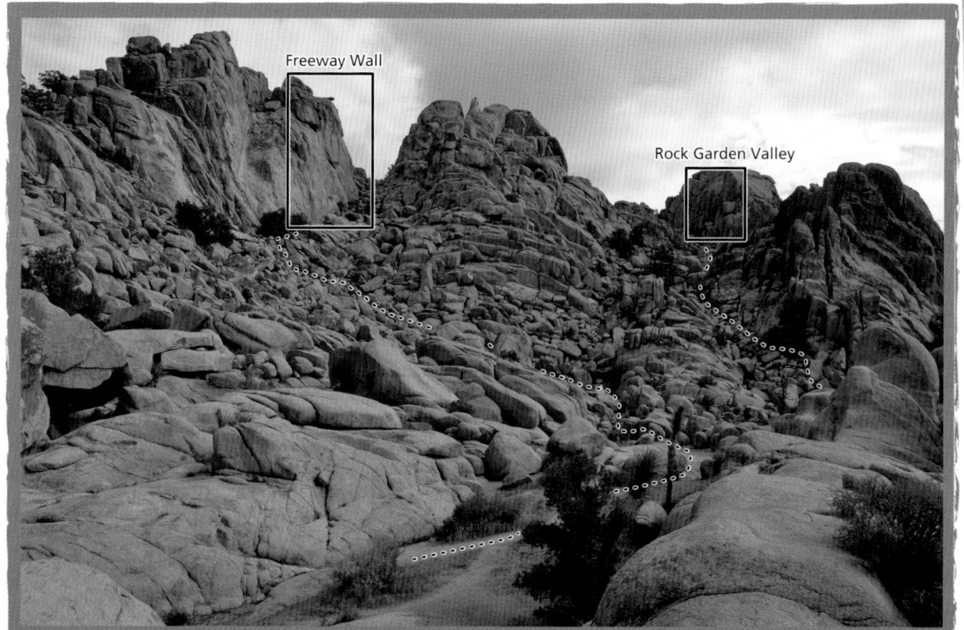

Descent: Head down the back (opposite) side and downclimb a short, exposed 4th-class section, then head right and circle back around, through a notch, and back to the base.

1. Sig Alert (5.10c) Begin on the left side of the face. Climb up to and over a corner (medium nuts), then climb the featured face on nice edges past five bolts to a 2-bolt anchor. The crux is at the fourth bolt. Above the last (fifth) bolt, the climbing is runout 5.7, but you can get additional pro with small stoppers if desired. **Descent:** Rappel 80 feet from the bolt anchor. **Pro:** stoppers from #1 to #6.

2. Nobody Walks in LA (5.9) A great variety of moves. This is the crack system just right of *Sig Alert* that leads all the way to the top. Gear anchor. **Pro:** to 3 inches.

3. Anacram (5.10c) Climb past a bolt to a corner, then move up to a second bolt and climb a steep, thin crack (crux). Gear anchor. **Pro:** to 3 inches.

4. Cakewalk (5.9) Great climbing with good pro. Start right of *Anacram* and climb a left-slanting crack for 30 feet, traverse left (height dependent), then climb up a vertical crack to the top. Gear anchor. **Pro:** to 3 inches.

Freeway Wall

Kyung Koh leading *Cakewalk* (5.9) on the Freeway Wall.
Photo Greg Epperson

ROCK GARDEN VALLEY

Wonderfully featured rock and a good variety of moderate cracks and face climbs characterize this area. It gets morning sun and afternoon shade. Getting to the cliff requires some strenuous scrambling but is well worth it.

Finding the crag: From the intersection of Park Boulevard and Lost Horse Road, drive 0.3 mile down Lost Horse Road and park on the left. Walk about 50 feet down the road (west) and turn left onto a hiking trail (GPS: N34° 01.425'/W116° 10.843'). Follow the trail for several hundred feet until it disappears into boulders. Scramble up through the boulders (3rd class), staying about 50 feet away from the wall to your right as you ascend the canyon. Hiking time to the cliff is about fifteen minutes. Crag GPS: N34° 01.315'/W116° 10.697'

Descent: All the climbs have bolted rappel anchors (less than 100 feet).

1. Young Lust (5.9-) A crack with good pro that climbs more like a face climb. Bolt anchor. **Pro:** to 3 inches.

2. Smithereens (5.9) The thin crack just right of *Young Lust*. Bolt anchor.

3. Rock Candy (5.9 + PG) Excellent face climbing. Traverse in from the left, then climb past two bolts to reach a vertical thin crack that peters out. Two more bolts protect face climbing to the top. Bolt anchor. **Descent:** Rappel from bolts at the top of Split Personality. *The bolts on top of Rock Candy/Double Dogleg are not set up for rappelling.* **Pro:** very thin to 1.5 inches.

4. Double Dogleg (5.7) A classic moderate hand crack with great jamming and good pro. 2-bolt anchor. **Descent:** Rappel from bolts at the top of Split Personality. *The bolts on top of*

Rock Garden Valley

Rock Candy/Double Dogleg are not set up for rappelling. **Pro:** to 3 inches.

5. Split Personality (5.9) Same start as Double Dogleg, then step right and climb a thin crack up to a bolted belay/rappel anchor. **Pro:** to 3 inches.

LOST HORSE WALL

The 400-foot-high Lost Horse Wall features Joshua Tree's best moderate multi-pitch trad routes. The wall receives early morning shade, then is in the sun for the rest of the day. In late spring the wall stays in the shade until about 11 a.m.

Finding the crag: From the intersection of Park Boulevard and Lost Horse Road, drive 0.4 mile down Lost Horse Road and park on the left (GPS N34° 01.333' / W116° 10.850'). Follow a trail for several hundred feet through a wash, then head left and scramble over boulders to the base of the wall. Hiking time is about six minutes. Crag GPS: N34° 01.259' / W116° 10.687'

Descent: From the top, head right (south) a few feet down a slab, then turn left and walk through a corridor/slot. Head right (south) and scramble down a few 3rd-class sections, eventually winding down and right to the base of the wall.

1. The Swift (5.7) Maybe the best 5.7 multi-pitch route in the park. **Pitch 1:** Begin from the left side of the wall.

Lost Horse Wall

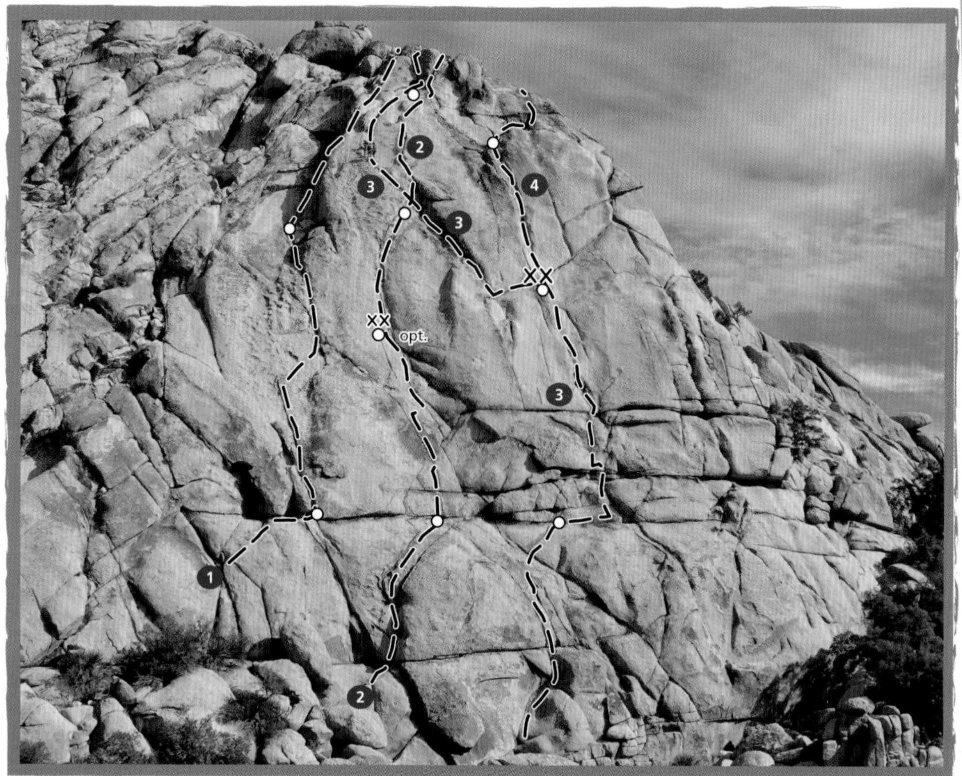

Climb up to a ledge and then traverse right to a prominent, jutting chockstone. Belay here. (A nice direct start [5.8 R] that leads directly up to the chockstone allows you to link pitches 1 and 2 with little rope drag, but the first pro is a ways up and the landing is bad.) **Pitch 2:** Follow the right of two cracks until you can face climb diagonally up and right to the prominent crack system that turns into a large left-facing corner. Follow the corner up to an area of blocks on ledges. The best belay anchor is at a small stance with a solid crack a few feet higher. **Pitch 3:** Climb up the corner until it steepens. When you are about 15 feet below an overhang in the corner, make a bold move onto the face to the right and climb up to a hand crack. Jam the crack (5.7, crux) until the climbing eases, then follow this crack system to the top. **Pro:** thin to 3 inches.

2. Bird on a Wire (5.10a) **Pitch 1:** Start about 50 feet left of Dappled Mare and climb easy cracks diagonally up and right to the big ledge and belay beneath a steeper headwall. **Pitch 2:** (5.10a) Make a move past a horizontal, then follow thin cracks up to a 2-bolt anchor (optional belay here, but you'll have hard moves right off the belay). Thin moves right above the anchor (5.9+/10a) lead to easier climbing up a juggy crack that slants slightly to the right. Belay where the route crosses *Dappled Mare* (or just below it to prevent a traffic jam if another party is on *Dappled Mare*). **Pitch 3:** Cross *Dappled Mare* and continue straight up on slabby cracks to a short right-slanting finger crack through a bulge (5.7) to the top. There is a good spot for an optional belay about 40 feet below the top. **Pro:** to 3 inches, including several extra 1.5- to 2.5-inch pieces.

3. Dappled Mare (5.8) **Pitch 1:** Start in the center of the face and climb easy cracks until you can move up and right on a slab up to a broad ledge. **Pitch 2:** From the right end of the ledge, climb up a few feet, step left, then follow a featured crack for over 100 feet up to a 3-bolt anchor. (Pitches 1 and 2 can be combined with a 60-meter rope, but watch rope drag.) **Pitch 3:** Climb down and left across the face/crack for about 20 feet (this is somewhat unprotected for the follower), then follow a left-leaning crack system that eventually slants back right and ends in a trough (optional belay here, 1.5- to 2.5-inch cams). Several finishes are possible. The best route climbs a right-slanting finger crack in a small corner (5.7) through a steeper section to the top. **Pro:** to 3 inches.

4. Roan Way (5.9-) This is an excellent and more direct finish to *Dappled Mare* that begins from the bolt belay of *Dappled Mare*'s second pitch. **Pitch 1:** Climb a steep chute directly above the belay (5.9-), exiting right after about 50 feet up to a nice ledge (gear anchor, 1.5 to 2.5 inches). **Pitch 2:** Move up and right from the ledge, crossing a steeper section at a horizontal crack (5.6), then climb up a low-angle crack on a slab (beware of loose rock here) to the top. **Pro:** to 2.5 inches.

4. Hemingway Buttress Area

The Hemingway Buttress area is a diverse area with many high-quality face and crack routes. Many of the climbs here are over 100 feet, which is long by Joshua Tree standards.

Getting there: From the West Entrance, drive 7.6 miles south on Park Boulevard and turn right into a large parking area with an outhouse. From the Intersection Rock Junction, drive 0.9 mile north and turn left (GPS: N34° 01.523' / W116° 10.498').

KEN BLACK MEMORIAL DOME

Just off the main park road, Blackjack climbs a varnished cliff that faces south, sheltered from north and west winds. The wall is in the sun in the morning and in the shade in the afternoon.

Finding the crag: From the West Entrance, drive 7.5 miles south and park at a small pullout on the right. If coming from the Intersection Rock Junction, drive 1.1 miles north to the pullout on the right (GPS: N34° 01.661' / W116° 10.572'). This pullout is just north of the larger Hemingway Buttress parking area. From the parking area, walk a few hundred feet to the northwest. Crag GPS: N34° 01.670' / W116° 10.642'

Hemingway Buttress Area

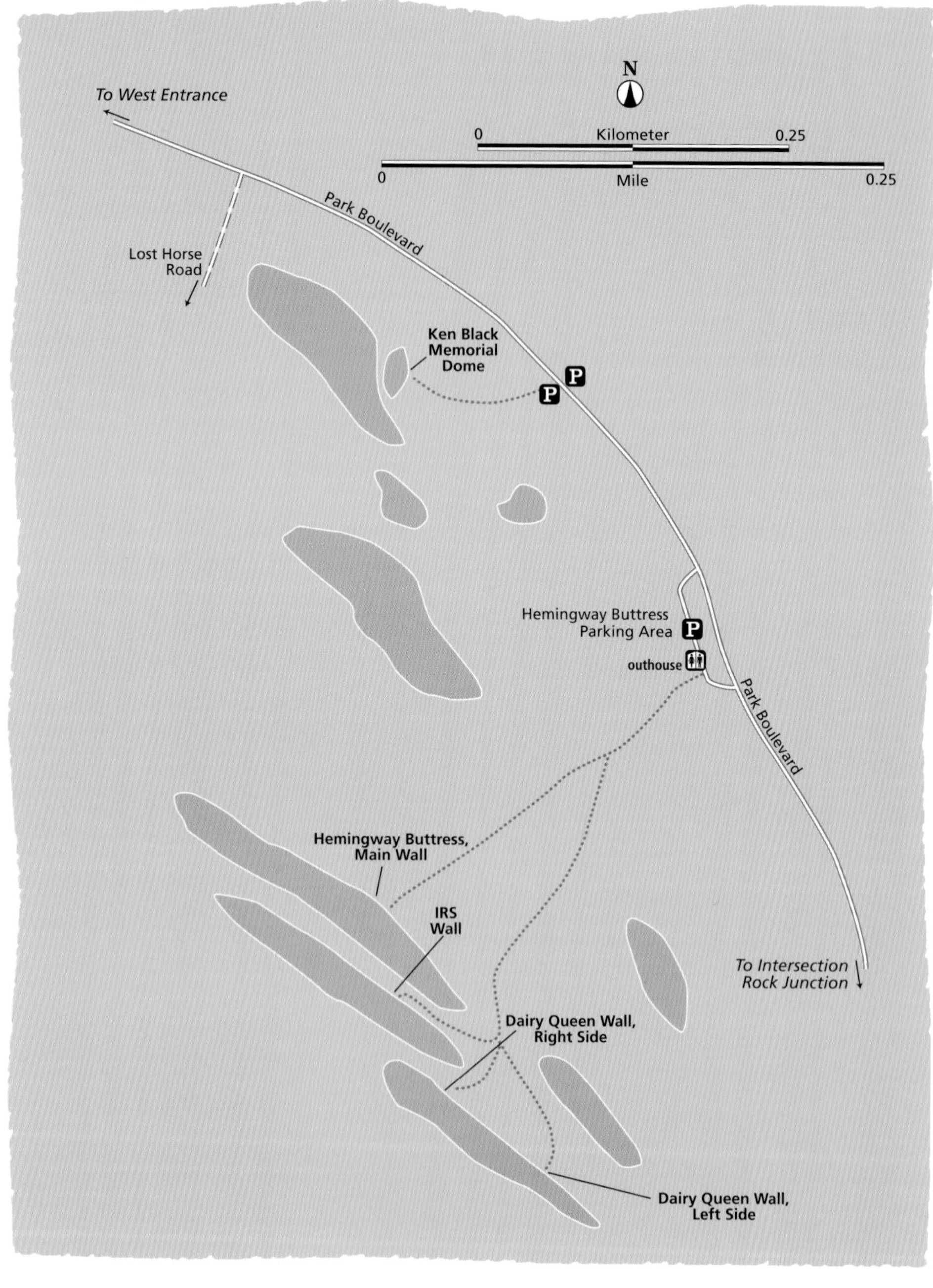

N
Kilometer
0
0.25
Mile
0
0.25
To West Entrance
Park Boulevard
Lost Horse Road
Ken Black Memorial Dome
P
P
Hemingway Buttress Parking Area
P
outhouse
Park Boulevard
Hemingway Buttress, Main Wall
IRS Wall
Dairy Queen Wall, Right Side
To Intersection Rock Junction
Dairy Queen Wall, Left Side

Ken Black Memorial Dome

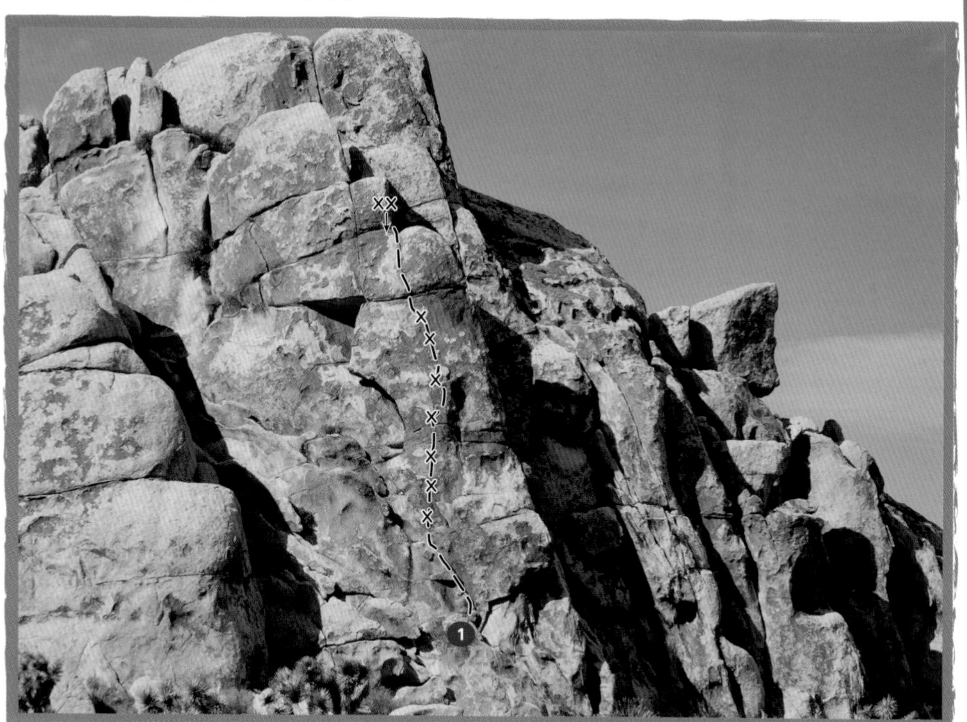

1. Blackjack (5.11a) Sport. Steep face climbing past seven bolts on nice patina. At the second bolt, move left, then back up (5.10b) and right to reach the third bolt. The crux is at the seventh bolt. **Descent:** 2-bolt lower-off anchor (80 feet). **Pro (optional):** Some cams from 2 to 4 inches can be used at the start and at the top to supplement the bolt protection if so desired.

HEMINGWAY BUTTRESS—MAIN WALL

This tall cliff faces east and gets morning sun and afternoon shade. The pitches are long and the rock quality is good. In late spring it does not get shade until around 1 p.m.

Finding the crag: From the Hemingway Buttress parking area, walk west for about 300 yards on a marked climber's trail, staying right where the trail forks. Crag GPS: N34° 01.449' / W116° 10.630'

Descent: Rappel with two ropes or one 70-meter rope (113 feet) from a bolt anchor near the top of *Poodles Are People Too,* or rap 80 feet from another set of bolts about 100 feet right of the finish of *Prepackaged.*

1. Overseer (5.9) (5.10a PG with direct start) The original start climbs an easy crack, then moves right to tackle the crux bulge. An excellent direct start begins just to the right and climbs the face via thin cracks up to the bulge. Gear anchor. **Pro:** thin to 3 inches, including extras from .75 to 2.5 inches. Bring a good selection of thin nuts and tiny cams for the direct start.

2. White Lightning (5.7+) A long pitch of classic jamming and face climbing. The crux is the first 30 feet. Gear anchor (1.5 to 2 inches). **Pro:** to 3 inches, including extra 1- to 2-inch pieces.

3. Poodles Are People Too (5.10b) Excellent face climbing that follows

Hemingway Buttress—Main Wall

During the first ascent of *Alf's Arête* in 1987, Alf Randelle hand-drilled the bolts in the traditional ground-up style prevalent at Joshua Tree at the time, using multiple ropes and tensioning off of hooks, taking several long falls in the process.

the thin crack and face just right of *White Lightning*. Bolt anchor. **Pro:** thin to 3 inches; bring a good selection of thin nuts.

4. Prepackaged (5.10a) Fun liebacking and jamming. The pro is good, but hard to place at the start. Gear anchor. **Pro:** thin nuts to a 4-inch cam.

IRS WALL

This cliff sits high on the hillside up and left from Hemingway Buttress's main cliff. It faces east and gets morning sun and afternoon shade.

Finding the crag: From the Hemingway Buttress parking area, walk west on the marked climber's trail and take the left fork, which leads to the base of a rocky hillside. Scramble up and right to get to the IRS Wall. Crag GPS: N34° 01.353' / W116° 10.606'

Descent: Both climbs have bolted rappel anchors (less than 100 feet).

IRS Wall and Dairy Queen Wall Overview

IRS Wall

1. Alf's Arête (5.11a PG) Excellent and exciting face climbing on thin edges. Climb past seven bolts to a 2-bolt belay/rappel anchor.

2. Taxman (5.10a/b) Steep, well-protected jamming. A Joshua Tree classic. The first part is the crux. 2-bolt belay/rappel anchor. **Pro:** to 3 inches.

Dairy Queen Wall—Right Side

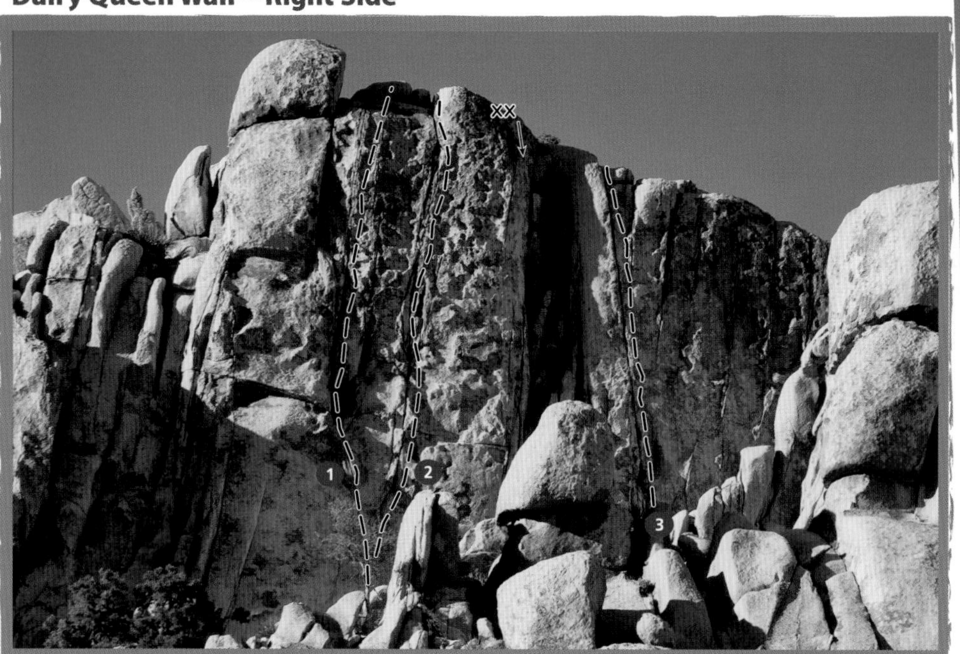

DAIRY QUEEN WALL—RIGHT SIDE

This very steep, bucketed cliff sits high on the hillside facing east. It gets morning sun and afternoon shade. In the winter this cliff gets very little sun.

Finding the crag: From the Hemingway Buttress parking area, walk west on the marked climber's trail and take the left fork, which leads to the base of a rocky hillside. Scramble up and right (some 4th class) to get to the upper Dairy Queen Wall. Crag GPS: N34° 01.339' / W116° 10.612'

Descent: Rappel from bolts near the top of *Mr. Misty Kiss,* or downclimb to the right.

1. Scrumdillyishus (5.7) Steep and exciting, with good pro. Climb the left branch of the crack, climbing through an alcove a bit higher. Gear anchor. **Pro:** to 3.5 inches.

2. Frosty Cone (5.7) Well-protected climbing up the right branch of the crack. Gear anchor. **Pro:** to 3.5 inches. The face to the right of *Frosty Cone* is a fun toprope (*Hot Fudge,* 5.9).

3. Mr. Misty Kiss (5.8) Climb the steep, left-slanting crack on the right side of the face. Gear anchor. **Pro:** to 3 inches.

DAIRY QUEEN WALL—LEFT SIDE

This cliff has some excellent slab climbs in addition to several classic cracks. It gets morning sun and afternoon shade. In the spring it stays in the sun until about 2 p.m. It is very sheltered from west winds.

Finding the crag: From the Hemingway Buttress parking area, walk west on the marked climber's trail and take the left fork, which leads to the base of a rocky hillside. Scramble (3rd class) over boulders (plus one low, short bouldery move) to get to the left side of the Dairy Queen Wall. Crag GPS: N34° 01.297' / W116° 10.597'

Descent: Rappel from bolt anchors (less than 100 feet).

1. Norm (5.10a) Undercling a flake (thin cams), then climb a knobby face and finish with a rounded arête. 2-bolt belay/rappel anchor. **Pro:** thin to 1.5 inches, five bolts, and a fixed rurp.

2. Leap Erickson (5.10b) Smear and edge your way up the slab past seven bolts to the top of *Leap Year Flake.* Gear anchor. **Descent:** Walk 50 feet right and rappel from a bolt anchor. **Pro:** to 3 inches.

3. Leap Year Flake (5.7) Jam a vertical crack, then move left and lieback a classic flake. Gear anchor. **Descent:** Walk 50 feet right and rappel from a bolt anchor. **Pro:** to 3 inches.

4. Adams Family (5.9) Climb a slabby crack past a bolt to a steeper section (crux), then follow the crack until you can move right to another crack and climb up to a 2-bolt belay/ rappel anchor (100 feet). **Pro:** thin to 3 inches. From the anchor you can also toprope *Gomez* (5.10a), the bolted line just to the right.

Dairy Queen Wall—Left Side

Dihedral Rock

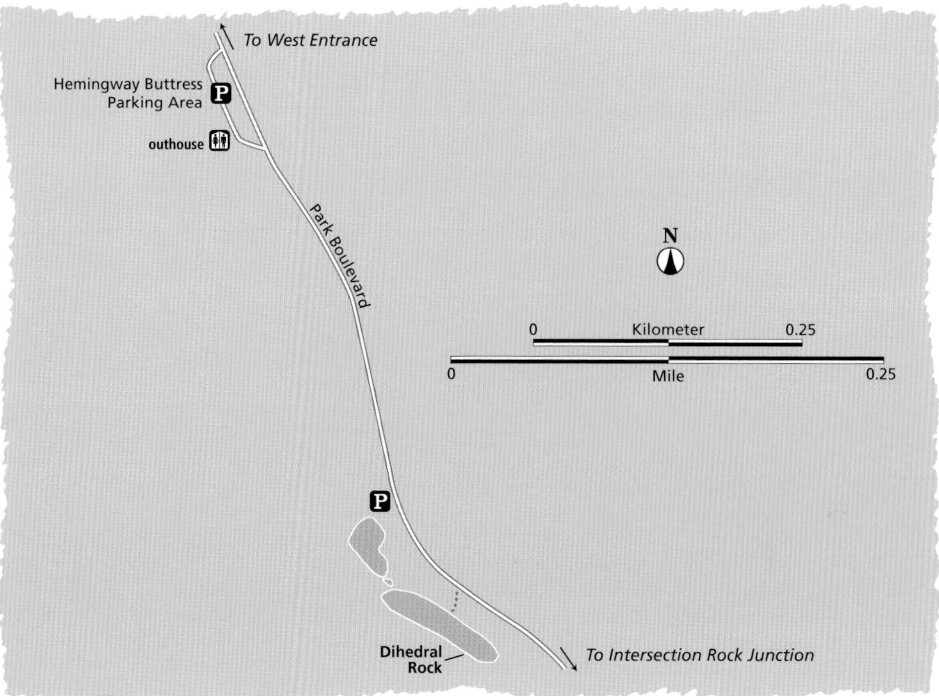

DIHEDRAL ROCK

The rock derives its name from Joshua Tree's most famous dihedral. It's one of the great stemming corners in the park.

Finding the crag: From the West Entrance, drive 7.9 miles south and park at a pullout on the right (just past the larger Hemingway Buttress parking area). From the Intersection Rock Junction, drive 0.6 mile north and park at the pullout on the left (GPS N34° 01.326' / W116° 10.388'). From the south end of the pullout, walk 200 feet along the road, then follow a marked climber's trail that leads directly to the rock. Crag GPS: N34° 01.197' / W116° 10.287'

Descent: Downclimb/scramble off the back then descend a steep gully to the right.

Nicky Dyal leads *Coarse and Buggy* (5.11b) on Dihedral Rock.
PHOTO GREG EPPERSON

Dihedral Rock

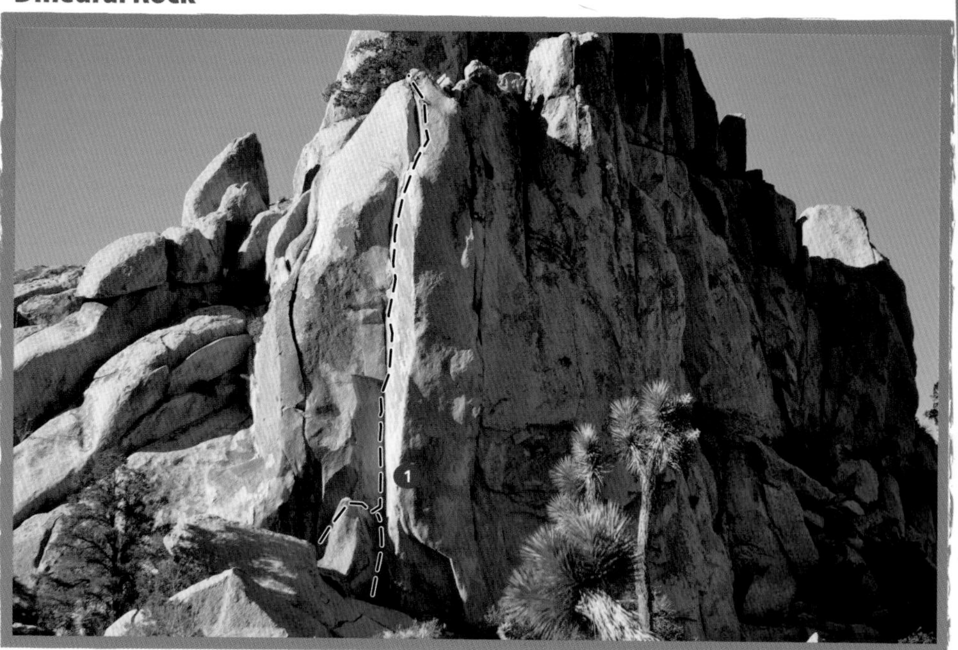

1. Coarse and Buggy (5.11b) Originally done by climbing into the corner from the block on the left. A direct start (5.10) climbs straight up from the base, but beware of loose rock. The crux (5.11b) involves intricate stemming up the corner, followed by another hard section of liebacking/jamming over the small roof near the top (5.10+). Some micro-nuts are very useful to protect the start. Gear anchor. **Pro:** to 3 inches.

Steven Powers leading *Right Ski Track* (5.10b) on Intersection Rock. Photo Greg Epperson

5.

Hidden Valley Campground

This area is the central hub of climbing activity in the park, and a traditional gathering and meeting spot for climbers. Hidden Valley Campground is the favored campsite by climbers due to its central location, stunning scenery, and proximity to major rock formations and bouldering areas.

Getting there: From the West Entrance, drive 8.6 miles into the park and turn left at a sign that reads Intersection Rock. Go about 200 feet to enter the large Intersection Rock parking area. GPS N34° 00.936′ / W116° 09.798′

Hidden Valley Campground

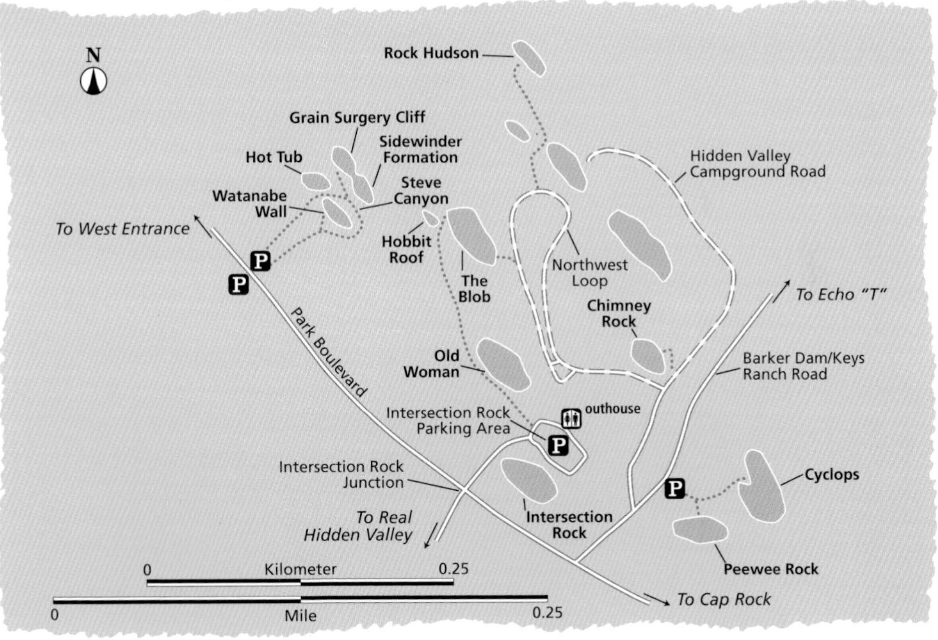

Hidden Valley Campground Overview

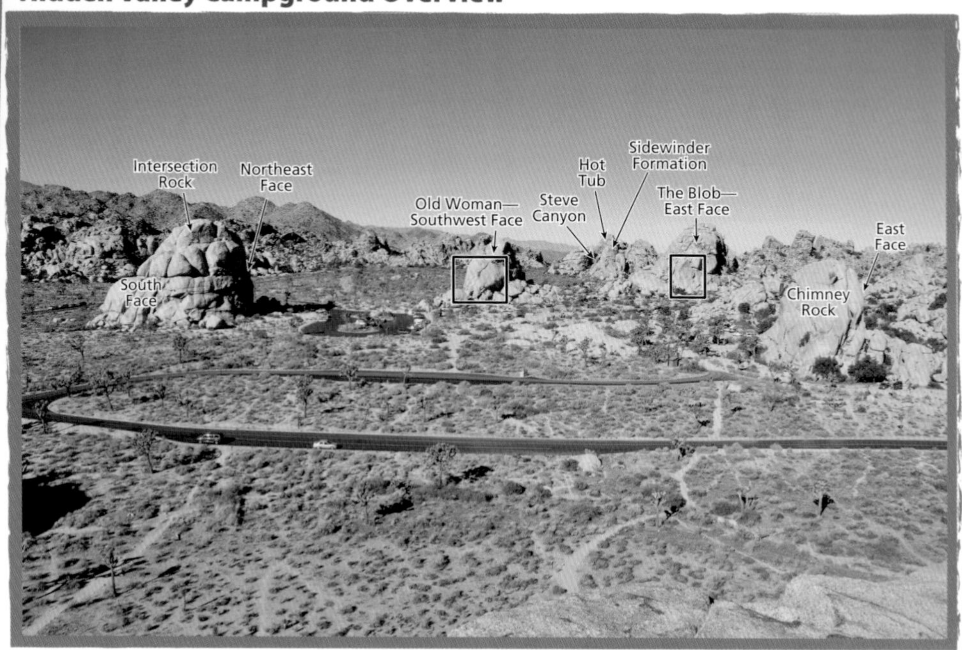

INTERSECTION ROCK

Encircled by parking lot and road, Intersection Rock rises like an island in the pavement, smack dab in the middle of the Joshua Tree climbing universe. The Intersection Rock parking lot serves as a central hub and meeting place for climbers. The intersection of the main road (Park Boulevard) and the turnoff to the Intersection Rock parking lot is used in this book as a marker (mile 0) to measure mileage to other areas, and is referred to as the "Intersection Rock Junction."

Finding the crag: Intersection Rock is the huge, domelike rock just south of the parking lot. From the parking lot you're looking at the northeast face. Crag GPS: N34° 00.936′ / W116° 09.798′

Descent: Rappel from bolts (85 feet) from the top of *North Overhang* down to the big ledge at the start of *Upper Right Ski Track,* then scramble down the west shoulder (3rd class). From the top of *Mike's Books,* you can make two single-rope (85 feet) raps from bolt anchors to the ground.

Intersection Rock—Northeast Face

Intersection Rock—Northeast Face

1. Left Ski Track (5.11b) One of John Bachar's favorite solos back in the day and a good testpiece for many climbers. Climb the strenuous, pocketed crack (crux) up to a bolt, then hand jam a deeper (5.9) crack to an easy (5.3) finish. **Pro:** to 3 inches.

2. Right Ski Track (5.10b) Climb steep pockets past a bolt through a bulge (crux), then climb a left-facing corner (5.8) up to a roof that is much easier than it looks. Gear anchor here; walk off to the right (3rd class) or continue to the top via *Upper Right Ski Track*. **Pro:** to 2.5 inches.

3. Upper Right Ski Track (5.1) Begin by scrambling up (3rd class) ledges on the right side to reach a large flat ledge. Face climb and stem your way up the corner. Some large cams are useful for the top anchor. **Pro:** to 4 inches.

Intersection Rock—South Face

1. Mike's Books (5.6) This old classic was one of the first routes climbed at Joshua Tree. **Pitch 1:** Start from the ledge on the far left and make a funky step-across to the right to enter the huge corner; the crux is where it steepens, then a groove leads to a huge ledge with a 2-bolt anchor (named Large Ledge). A direct start to this pitch can be done up the short hand crack (5.8+) **Pitch 2:** Climb the huge flake that sits at the base of the dihedral, then stem and chimney about 30 feet up the corner until you can make an improbable move out left onto a slabby face. Move back right and follow the crack until it peters out, then step over a bulge onto a low-angle face, clipping a bolt where it steepens (5.5) near the top. 2-bolt belay/rappel anchor. **Pro:** to 3.5 inches; a large cam or two are handy for the dihedral on pitch 2.

2. The Waterchute (5.10b) A test-piece in the old days. Rarely led, but easily toproped from the *Mike's Books* anchor. It's the archetypical Joshua Tree flared chimney that is both strenuous and slippery. The entry move can be done with either a flying leap or by face climbing. Bolt anchor. **Descent:** Rappel 80 feet. **Pro:** one bolt, gear to 3 inches.

3. Shauna Grant (5.10d) Short and sweet. Climb the steep face of a block past four bolts to a 2-bolt anchor. **Descent:** Downclimb the chimney just left (easy 5th class) back to the big ledge.

Intersection Rock—South Face

Shauna Grant was a rising star of pornographic films in the early 1980s whose meteoric career was tragically cut short at the age of twenty by a self-inflicted gunshot wound in Palm Springs, California.

Intersection Rock—West Face

1. Overhang Bypass (5.7) **Pitch 1:** Begin by climbing the middle of three cracks, up to a cavelike overhang. Make a wild stemming maneuver to cross over to the right, onto the face, about 15 feet below the overhang. Climb up, then left on a slab to reach a lieback flake, which is followed up to a big sloping ledge. Gear anchor. You can also climb straight up over the overhang (5.9) or bypass it on the left side (5.6). **Pitch 2:** Make an intimidating, hard-to-protect hand traverse right out the overhang, then climb a slab past one bolt to the top. 2-bolt anchor on top. **Pro:** to 2.5 inches.

2. North Overhang (5.9) **Pitch 1:** Climb the first pitch of *Overhang Bypass.* **Pitch 2:** Climb left past a bolt to reach a crack that leads around the left side of the big overhang. 2-bolt anchor on top.

3. The Flake (5.8) Climb a wide, flaring chimney, then follow a long crack system up to a friction face with two bolts. There is an optional belay at a nice stance (gear anchor, 1 to 3 inches) on a narrow ledge below the friction face if you'd like less rope drag. **Pro:** to 3 inches, including a double set of cams from 1.5 to 2.5 inches.

Intersection Rock—West Face

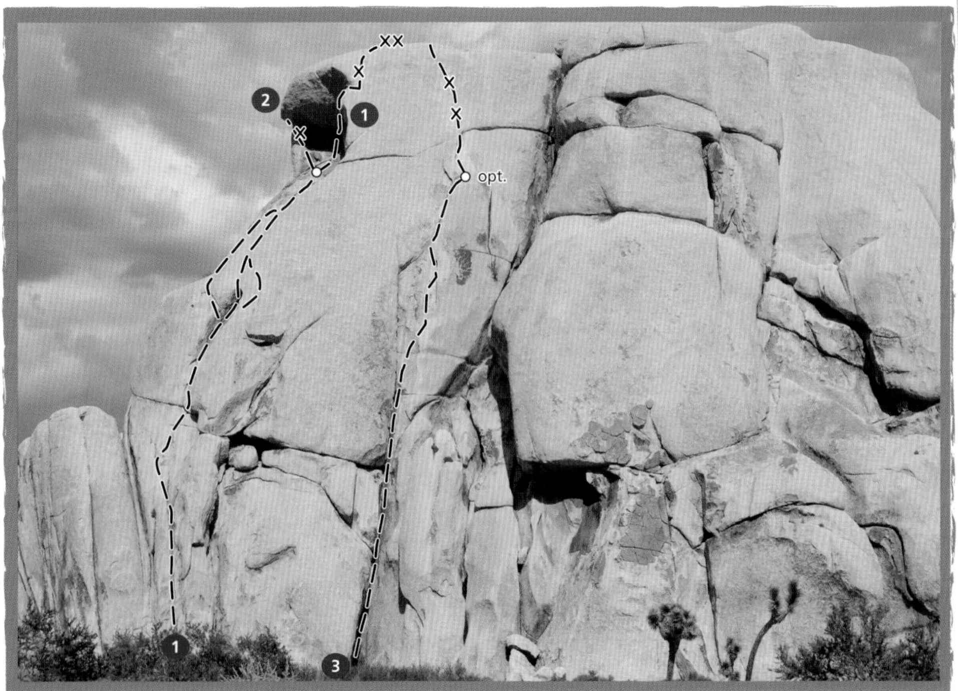

Bird Lew with a bird's-eye view on the must-do route *North Overhang* (5.9), Intersection Rock.
PHOTO GREG EPPERSON

OLD WOMAN

This quintessential roadside crag is riddled with classic crack climbs in the 5.7 to 5.10a range. It sees plenty of action, particularly on weekends.

Finding the crag: This large formation is located 200 feet northwest of the Intersection Rock parking lot and is in the sun most of the day. Crag GPS: N34° 00.973' / W116° 09.825'

Descent: Several bolted rap stations (less than 100 feet) facilitate descent.

Old Woman—West Face

1. Dogleg (5.9-) Begin from the right with a delicate face move to enter the corner, then stem, jam, and lieback your way up the awesome crack. 100 feet. Gear anchor. **Descent:** Top out, then downclimb (4th class) a flake on the opposite side 20 feet down to a ledge. Rappel (less than 100 feet) from a bolt anchor. **Pro:** medium to large stoppers and cams from 1 to 3 inches, including extras from 1 to 1.25 inches.

2. Double Cross (5.8) Classic hand jamming in a long vertical crack. An optional 4-inch cam protects the face climbing up to a scoop, then jam the long vertical crack that ends with a few chimney moves at the top. 2-bolt belay/rappel anchor. **Pro:** to 4 inches, including a double set of cams from 2 to 3 inches.

> *Double Cross* has been the scene of more leader fall accidents than any other route in the park. Be competent in trad leading, jamming, and protection skills before taking on this climb.

Old Woman—West Face

3. Sexy Grandma (5.9-) Sport. A popular climb with a variety of fun moves. Start with a flared chimney, then step right and climb up to an overhang. Make a classic move out the left side of the overhang, then friction up a rounded arête to an easy crack. 2-bolt lower-off anchor (less than 100 feet). **Pro:** three bolts and two fixed pins, optional 2- to 3-inch cams.

4. Bandsaw (5.10c R) Great climbing, but a very bold lead. Easily toproped off the *Sexy Grandma* anchor. Start on a pointed boulder with a thin reach left to an unprotected mantle (5.10 R with a bad landing) to reach the first bolt. Thin edging leads up to an overhang. Move right, then up a friction slab to the top. **Pro:** three bolts, plus a 1- to 2-inch piece under the roof.

5. Orphan (5.9+) Stem up the corner, jam a hand crack, then climb a squeeze chimney to the top. Gear anchor. **Descent:** Rappel from bolts right of *Toe Jam*. **Pro:** to 4 inches, including several from 3 to 4 inches.

6. Dandelion (5.10a) Climb a right-arching crack, jam a vertical hand crack (crux), then climb the face past a bolt to the top. Gear anchor. **Descent:** Rappel from bolts right of *Toe Jam*. **Pro:** to 3 inches.

Hidden Valley Campground Overview

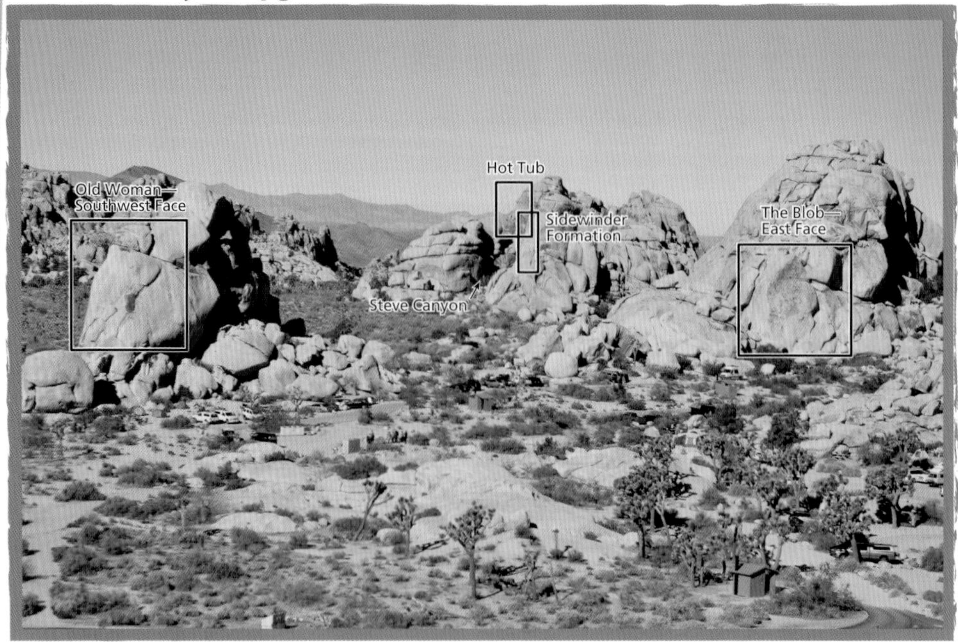

Old Woman—Southwest Face

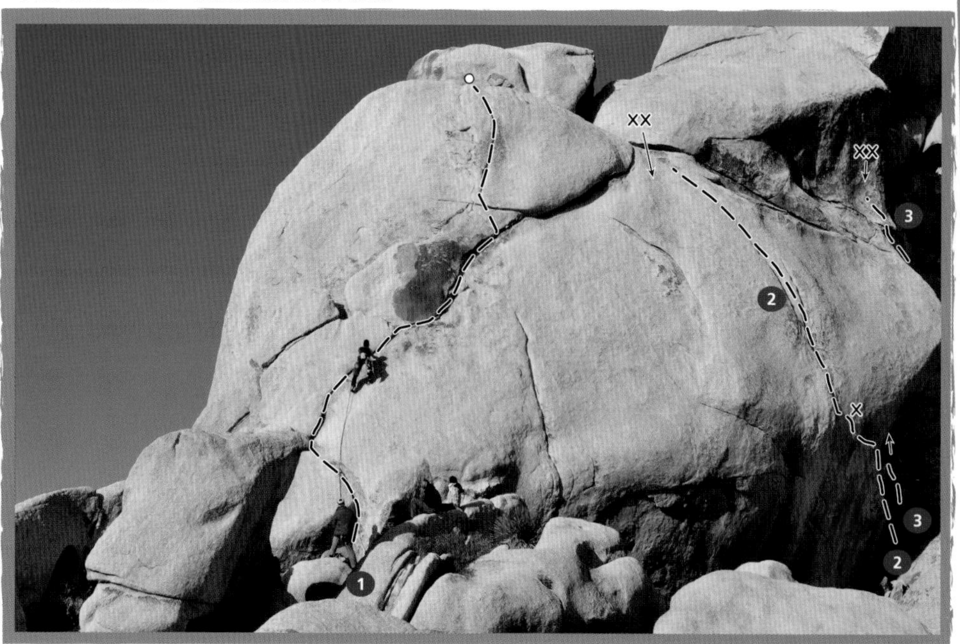

Old Woman—Southwest Face

1. Toe Jam (5.7) A campground classic and a standard for the grade. Start with a stem to a lieback/jam. Follow the flake system up to the "toe jam" finish. Gear anchor. **Descent:** Rappel from bolts about 20 feet to the right. **Pro:** to 3 inches.

2. Bearded Cabbage (5.10c) Very gymnastic. Hand traverse left to a bolt, then heel hook and make a big reach left to a crack, which is followed to the top. The crux is easier if you have big ape index. **Pro:** 1 to 3 inches.

3. Spider Line (5.11d) This campground testpiece is both technical and strenuous. Jam, stem, and lieback the overhanging dihedral to a 2-bolt belay/rappel anchor. **Pro:** to 2.5 inches. You can access the anchor for toproping with a short traversing pitch from the *Toe Jam* rappel bolts (5.8).

THE BLOB

This is the huge, amorphous formation on the northwest side of Hidden Valley Campground.

Finding the crag: Park at Intersection Rock parking lot. To get to The Blob's northwest face, walk to the left of the *Old Woman formation—The Blob* will be the next formation immediately to the north. Continue walking along the left (west) side of *The Blob* to reach the northwest face. To reach the east face routes, walk into the northwest campground loop—*The Blob* is the next formation past the *Old Woman* on the left. The east face routes are behind campsite 21. GPS coordinates are included with individual route and cliff face descriptions.

The Blob—Northwest Face

1. Hobbit Roof (5.10c) A fun little gem that's easy to toprope. Crimp past a bolt on a slab (5.10c), then jam a thin hand crack over a small roof. (5.9) Gear anchor (3-inch cams). You can avoid the tough slab move by climbing in from the right. It's easy to rig a toprope by scrambling around the left side (3rd class) to the top. Route GPS: N34 01.106' / W116 09.901'

2. The Bong (5.5) Approach via a chute (3rd class) just right of *Hobbit Roof.* A classic moderate climb with good pro and some nice hand jams. Gear anchor. Route GPS: N34 01.122' / W116 09.878'. **Descent:** Head northwest a few feet (toward the campground), then down a chimney on the left. Fourth-class scrambling takes you to a chasm at the base of the cliff; tunnel and chimney back over to the start. **Pro:** to 3 inches.

The Blob—Northwest Face

Beth Renn leading *Hobbit Roof* (5.10c), The Blob. Photo Greg Epperson

The Blob—East Face

This face is directly above campsite 21 on the northwest campground loop. Crag GPS: N34° 01.078' / W116° 09.825'. **Occupied campsite rule:** If campers are in this site, please ask their permission before climbing these routes.

Descent: Scramble a few feet west, then downclimb a chimney (easy 5th class) to reach a gully that leads back left to the base. You can also make an awkward rappel from slings on a block at the top of *Mama Woolsey* (80 feet).

1. Buissonier (5.8-) Lieback, jam, and chimney up the crack. Strenuous to place gear on the lead. Some large

Royal Robbins made the first ascent of Buissonier in 1965.

cams are useful for the top anchor (2 to 3 inches). **Pro:** to 3 inches.

2. Papa Woolsey (5.10b/c) Considered to be Joshua Tree's first sport climb, albeit without a bolt anchor! **Pro:** six bolts plus some cams for the top anchor (2 to 3 inches).

3. Mama Woolsey (5.10a R) Start just right of *Papa Woolsey* with a face move up to a right-slanting crack. When the crack peters out, move right on delicate friction (5.10a R),

The Blob—East Face

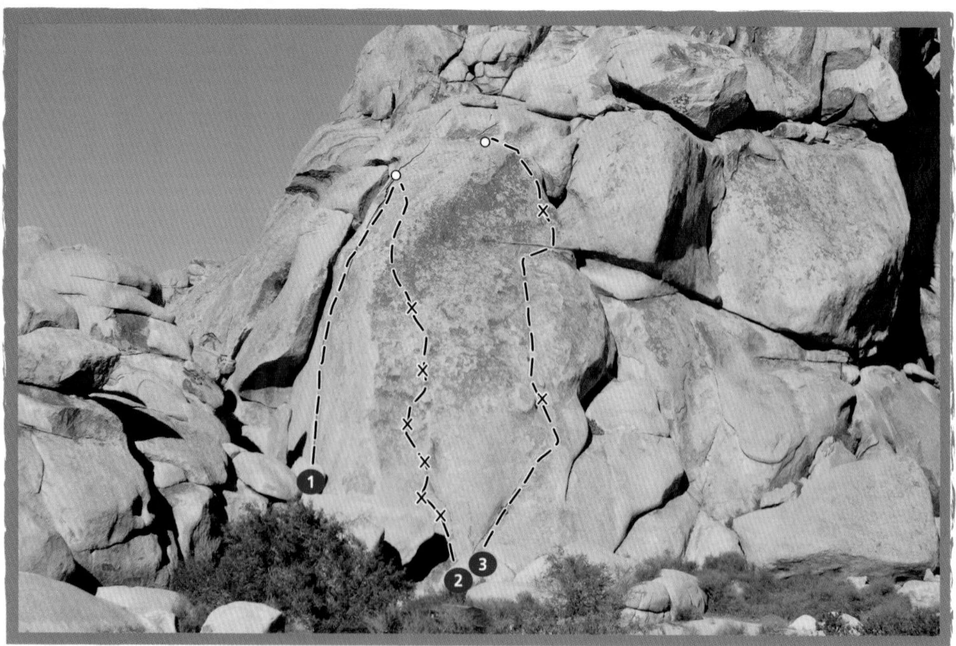

First climbed in 1972, *Papa Woolsey* is considered to be Joshua Tree's first sport climb, although in the quirky Joshua Tree definition: a route with bolt protection, a gear anchor, and downclimb descent. Originally rated 5.9, it has become thinner and more difficult with disappearing edges and polished smears.

then up to a bolt. Follow an easier thin crack up the slab, move right over an overlap, then up the final slab past one more bolt. Gear anchor. **Pro:** .5 to 2.5 inches.

ROCK HUDSON

This striking formation has an impressive southwest face with one of Joshua Tree's top ten climbs. It gets morning shade and afternoon sun.

Finding the crag: From the Intersection Rock parking lot, walk to the north end of the northwest campground loop road, then go north, behind campsite 16, heading to the right of a large, pointed rock formation and through a gap, where you'll see Rock Hudson as the largest formation 200 yards to the north. Crag GPS: N34° 01.273' / W116° 09.783'

1. Hot Rocks (5.11b/c) A stupendous finger to hand crack on an impressive wall. Thin face climbing (5.10+) past a bolt gains entry to the crack. **Descent:** Scramble down to the right (south shoulder). **Pro:** to 3 inches.

Rock Hudson

Watanabe Wall/Hot Tub Formation Overview

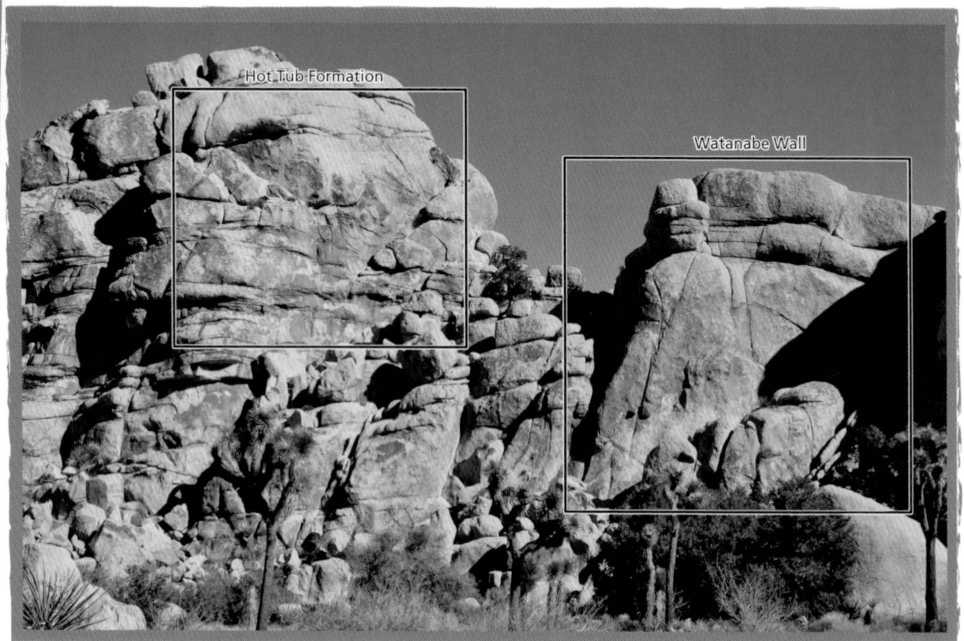

WATANABE WALL

This west-facing wall has a classic crack climb just minutes from the main park road.

Finding the crag: From the West Entrance, drive 8.3 miles and park at a large pullout on the left. From the Intersection Rock Junction, drive 0.3 mile north and park on the right (GPS: N34° 01.106′ / W116° 10.085′). From the pullout, take the right of two marked climber's trails. Walk east on the trail for about 300 feet directly to the formation. Crag GPS: N34° 01.102′ / W116° 09.047′

Roadrunner

Watanabe Wall

1. Watanabe Wall (5.10a) Climb a flake up to a vertical crack (jamming crux) up to where the crack forks. From here you can go left (5.8) (with an optional exit and walk-off to the left) or take the right branch (5.9). 2-bolt belay/rappel anchor (30-foot rappel off the back side). **Descent:** The easiest descent is to scramble (3rd class) off the back side down into Steve Canyon, then walk right (south) and around the formation back to the base. You can also head down toward the road (west) from the base of the Hot Tub formation, but this involves a bit of 4th-class downclimbing. **Pro:** to 4 inches.

HOT TUB FORMATION

This formation boasts three steep face climbs on a sunny, south-facing cliff that is sheltered from north winds. The cliff is in the sun most of the day.

Finding the crag: From the West Entrance, drive 8.3 miles and park at a large pullout on the left. From the Intersection Rock Junction, drive 0.3 mile north and park on the right (GPS N34° 01.106' / W116° 10.085'). The easiest approach is via Steve Canyon. From the pullout, take the right of two marked climber's trails. Walk east on the trail and follow it around to the right of a large rock formation to reach Steve Canyon. The Sidewinder Cliff is on the right as you enter Steve Canyon. Go past the Sidewinder formation, then head up the left side of the canyon until you can scramble (3rd class) up the canyon's left wall. You can also access the wall by hiking directly east from the pullout (take the left of the two marked climber's trails), but this involves a bit of 4th-class maneuvering to reach the base. Crag GPS: N34° 01.148' / W116° 10.017'

1. Elixer (5.10b) Begin from a block on the left side of the face. Climb the steep wall past three bolts and several horizontal cracks up to a 2-bolt belay/rappel anchor. (From this anchor you can also toprope the crack directly below: *Dharma Bums,* 5.9) **Pro:** two 1.5-inch cams (#1 camalots) for the two horizontal cracks above the last bolt.

2. Amanda (5.10a) Wonderful in its variety. Begin about 30 feet right of *Elixer* and just right of a vertical crack (*Dharma Bums,* 5.9). Stretch to clip a bolt, power up the steep face past several horizontal cracks, then stem, mantle, and friction past four more

Hot Tub Formation

bolts up to a 2-bolt belay/rappel anchor. **Pro:** five bolts, medium nuts, cams to 2 inches.

3. We Never Get the Girls (5.10b) Start 15 feet right of *Amanda* and climb up to a ledge, then step left and climb the face past four bolts up to a 2-bolt belay/rappel anchor. Beware of some loose rock above the second bolt. **Pro:** to 2 inches.

SIDEWINDER CLIFF

This cliff, located at the entrance to Steve Canyon, faces west and gets morning shade, then afternoon sun.

Finding the crag: From the West Entrance, drive 8.3 miles and park at a large pullout on the left. From the Intersection Rock Junction, drive 0.3 mile north and park on the right (GPS: N34° 01.106' / W116° 10.085'). From the pullout, take the right of two marked climber's trails. Walk east on the trail and follow it around to the right of a large rock formation to reach Steve Canyon. The Sidewinder formation is on the right as you enter Steve Canyon. Crag GPS: N34° 01.114' / W116° 09.969'

Descent: Jump across to the little tower on the left (northwest), then rappel from two bolts.

1. Jumping Jack Crack (5.11b) Climb a flared chimney (5.9), then jam a thin hand crack through a bulge to exit. **Pro:** .4 to 3 inches plus a big cam or two (4 to 6 inches) for the chimney.

2. Sidewinder (5.10b PG/R) Exciting to lead, but not for the faint of heart! A bolt protects a long reach (5.10-) to a left-arching crack. Climb up to another bolt, then tiptoe left (scary 5.10b) across the dike to the top. Gear anchor. **Pro:** to 3.5 inches.

Sidewinder Cliff

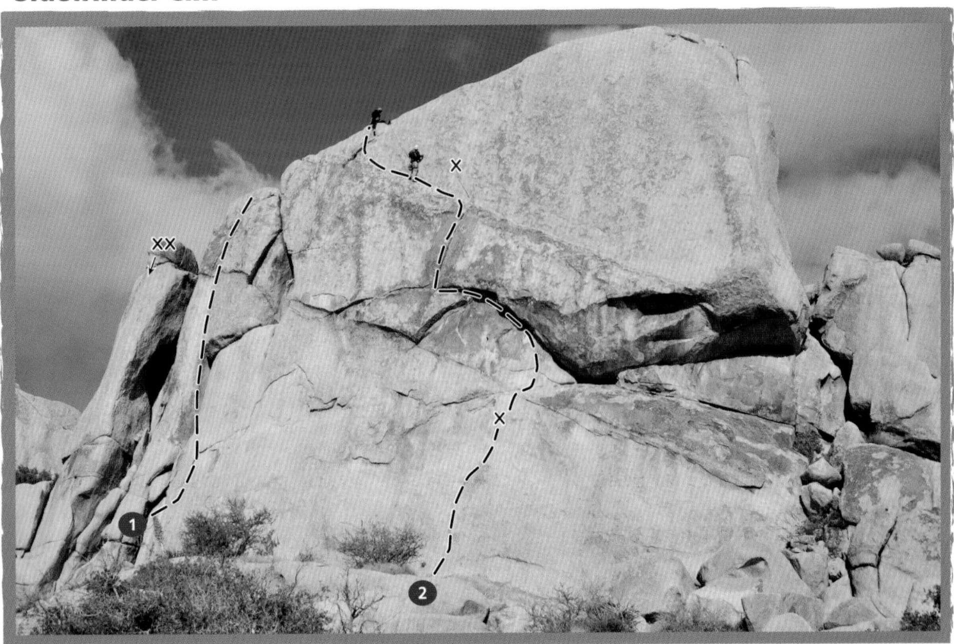

GRAIN SURGERY CLIFF

This cliff is in the shade in the early morning, then in the sun most of the day, and is somewhat sheltered from west winds.

Finding the crag: From the West Entrance, drive 8.3 miles and park at a large pullout on the left. From the Intersection Rock Junction, drive 0.3 mile north and park on the right (GPS: N34° 01.106'/ W116° 10.085'). From the pullout, take the right of two marked climber's trails. Walk east on the trail and follow it around to the right of a large rock formation to reach Steve Canyon. The Grain Surgery Cliff is on the right side of the canyon, about 200 feet past the Sidewinder formation. Crag GPS: N34° 01.145'/ W116° 09.993'

1. Grain Surgery (5.10b PG/R) Jam a vertical crack, then move left and up a slab (5.10b) past two bolts to the top. 2-bolt belay/rappel anchor (80 feet). **Pro:** to 2.5 inches.

2. The Decompensator of Lhasa (5.10d PG) Step off a boulder and climb a left-arching crack (5.8), then up and right on incredible face climbing (5.10+) past four bolts to the top. Gear anchor. **Descent:** Rappel *Grain Surgery*. **Pro:** to 2.5 inches.

Grain Surgery Cliff

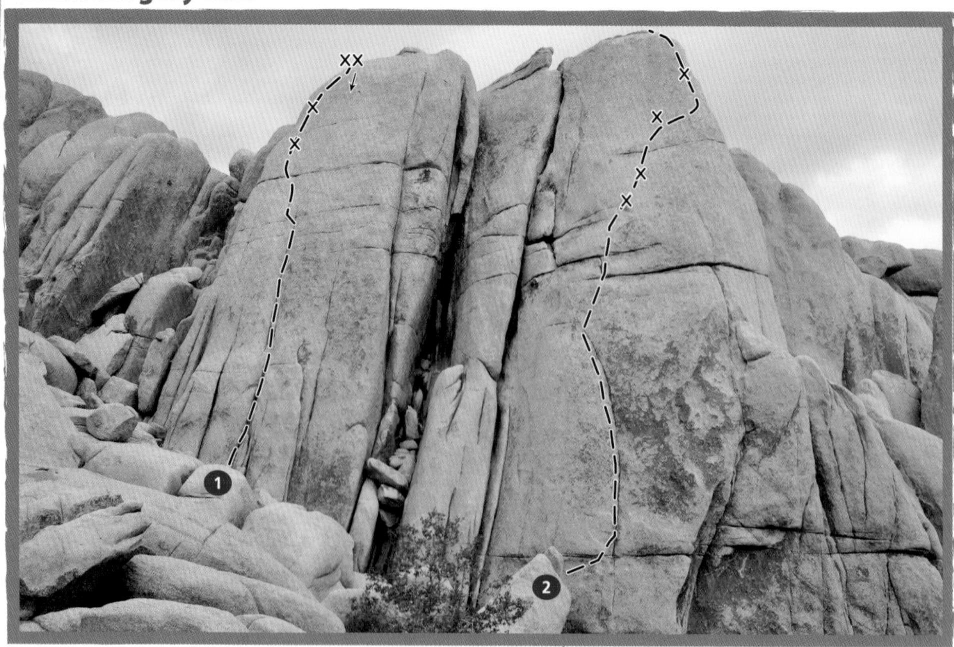

CHIMNEY ROCK

This large dome of rock rises in the middle of Hidden Valley Campground. The east face is in the sun in the morning, then in the shade all afternoon.

Finding the crag: From the Intersection Rock parking lot, this is the large dome 150 yards to the northeast, adjacent to campsite 32. Crag GPS: N34° 01.006' / W116° 09.671'

Descent: Rappel 80 feet from bolts.

1. The Flue (5.8+) Decipher funky face moves (crux), then move left and follow the juggy, right-leaning crack to the top. 2-bolt belay/rappel anchor. **Descent:** Rappel less than 100 feet. **Pro:** to 4 inches.

2. Blind Ambition (5.11a or 5.10a) Start about 40 feet right of *The Flue.* Climb past a bolt to a horizontal crack (5.10), hand traverse right, then smear up a steep slab (5.11-) past two bolts to an easier (5.10a) move past a third bolt over a bulge. Easier face climbing leads to the top. 2-bolt belay/rappel anchor. You can toprope a 5.10a route by climbing the finger crack just to the right (5.9), avoiding the 5.11 crux by bypassing it to the right, then moving left to rejoin the route for its normal finish.

Chimney Rock—East Face

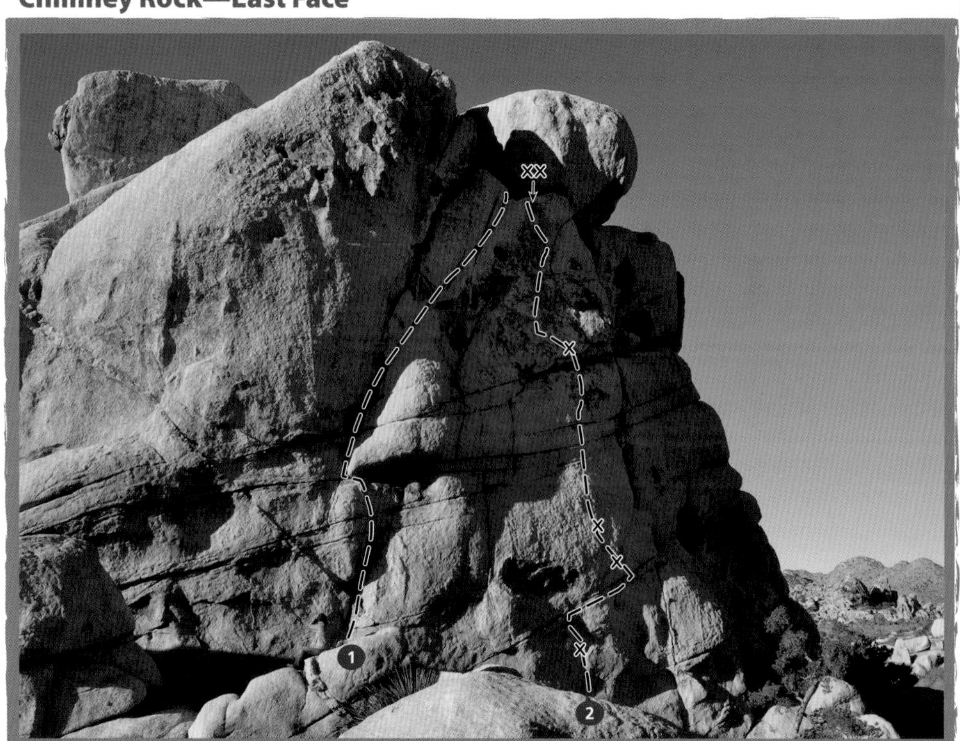

CYCLOPS

This is the large formation with the flat mesalike summit, easily seen to the southeast from the Intersection Rock parking lot. The "eye" is a hole through the center of the rock at the very top. *The Eye* route finishes through this tunnel. The climbs are in the shade in the morning and the sun in the afternoon.

Finding the crag: This crag is located about 100 yards to the south of Hidden Valley Campground. From the Intersection Rock Junction, drive south for 0.1 mile, turn left at the Barker Dam/Keys Ranch Road, drive 0.1 mile, and park on the right (GPS: N34° 00.900' / W116° 09.662'). There is a marked climber's trail that leads directly to the Cyclops formation. Crag GPS: N34° 00.901' / W116° 09.585'

Descent: Third class down the opposite (east) side. From the summit area, scramble southeast, down slabs, staying left to avoid steeper terrain, then back right on slabs to more scrambling through boulders.

1. The Eye (5.5 PG) Climb an easy trough, then move a bit right onto a steeper face with large holds, angle back left, then straight up over a steep bulge. Easier climbing leads up to and through the "eye." Gear anchor. **Pro:** to 3.5 inches. Some large cams are useful for the anchor (3 to 3.5 inches). This climb is in the shade until the afternoon.

Cyclops—West Face

Cyclops—West Face, Right Side

2. The Official Route of the 1984 Olympics (5.10d) Great face climbing with a contrast of delicate smearing to a powerful reach at the crux. Bolt anchor on top (110 feet). **Descent:** Sling the bolts for rappelling, or do the 3rd-class descent. **Pro:** five bolts, gear to 2.5 inches. You can toprope this route with a 70-meter rope.

PEEWEE ROCK

Peewee Rock has a fun sport climb with a very short approach. It faces north, so it is in the shade most of the time.

Finding the crag: This crag is located about 100 yards to the south of Hidden Valley Campground. From the Intersection Rock Junction, drive south for 0.1 mile, turn left at the Barker Dam/Keys Ranch Road, drive 0.1 mile, and park on the right (GPS N34° 00.900' / W116° 09.662'). A marked climber's trail leads to the rock. Crag GPS: N34° 00.868' / W116° 09.634'

1. Peewee's Piton (5.10a) Sport. Start with a crux reach over a bulge, then make tricky moves up a left-slanting seam. Step over another bulge (5.8) to easier climbing. 2-bolt lower-off anchor (80 feet). **Pro:** seven bolts, optional 1-inch cam above the second bolt. From the anchor you can toprope *Oui Oui* (5.10d PG/R), the 4-bolt face just to the right.

> Peewee's Piton was named after the infamous Pee wee Herman. The original first point of pro was an angle piton in a drilled hole, but it has since been replaced with a glued-in eyebolt.

Peewee Rock

6.

Real Hidden Valley

Formerly a cattle rustler's hangout, today the Real Hidden Valley has one of the park's most popular nature trails (a 1-mile loop trail), and some of the park's best climbing.

Getting there: From the West Entrance, drive 8.6 miles into the park and turn right at a sign that reads HIDDEN VALLEY PICNIC AREA (this is the Intersection Rock Junction). Drive 0.2 mile to large parking area and trailhead for the Hidden Valley Nature Trail (GPS: N34° 00.743' / W116° 10.083').

Real Hidden Valley

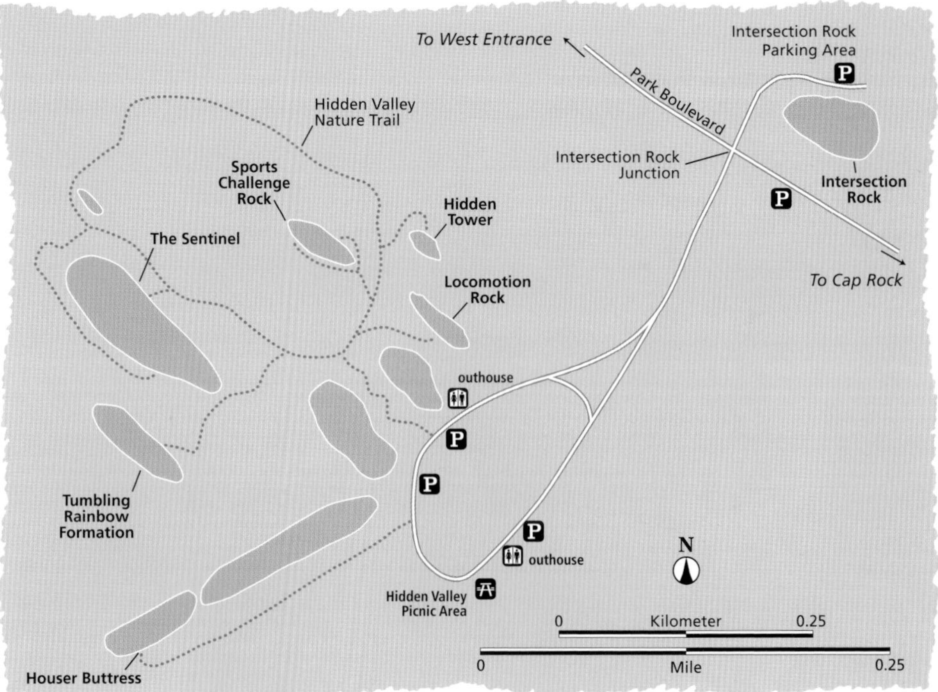

TUMBLING RAINBOW FORMATION

This is the towering formation that sits high on the west side of the Real Hidden Valley. The climbs have excellent rock quality, and there is a wonderful view of the park from the summit.

Finding the crag: Walk the Hidden Valley Nature Trail for about 300 feet to the nature trail's loop junction. Tumbling Rainbow can be seen as the highest formation about 350 yards to the southwest. Go left at the nature trail loop and walk about 100 feet, then cut left off the nature trail and follow a climber's trail through boulders to the base of the cliff, which is most easily approached from the left via a short 4th-class scramble. Crag GPS: N34° 00.740′ / W116° 10.276′

Descent: Two separate bolted rappel anchors are located at the top of *Runaway* and *Days of Thunder* (80 feet).

1. Runaway (5.11b) Sport. Begin with steep and powerful moves (crux 5.11-), then traverse left and follow an incredible series of edges that lead to a friction finish. 10 bolts to a 2-bolt anchor.

2. Run For Your Life (5.10b PG) One of the classic 5.10 Joshua Tree face routes. Start with unprotected 5.9 (a bit off the deck with a hard landing) to reach the first bolt. Another runout (5.7) gets you to the second bolt.

Tumbling Rainbow Formation

Some great edges lead to sustained slab moves and an exciting finish. **Pro:** six bolts (bring a long runner for the fifth bolt). Some medium nuts or cams are needed for a gear anchor directly above the finish—the belay/rappel bolts at the top of *Runaway* are off to the side.

3. Tumbling Rainbow (5.9) Jam a left-slanting hand crack, then follow the wide crack (easier than it looks because you can stem it) to the top. **Pro:** to 4 inches.

4. Tonic Boom (5.12a PG) Start with a thin crack up to a bolt. Traverse left on a flake to a bolt, then climb the intimidating face past one more bolt up to a 2-bolt belay/rappel anchor. **Pro:** thin to .75 inch.

5. Days of Thunder (5.11b) Start with a thin crack up to a tricky crux move at a bolt. Move left from the crack (medium stopper) and climb the face/arête past three bolts (5.10b). 2-bolt belay/rappel anchor. **Pro:** thin to .75 inch.

6. Fisticuffs (5.10b) A very short but clean Yosemite-like splitter that begins as a hand crack and widens to fist jams. Where the crack goes horizontal, you can belay with large cams and then scramble off to the right (north). **Descent:** Scramble off to the right. **Pro:** 2.5 to 4.5 inches, including doubles from 3 to 4.5 inches.

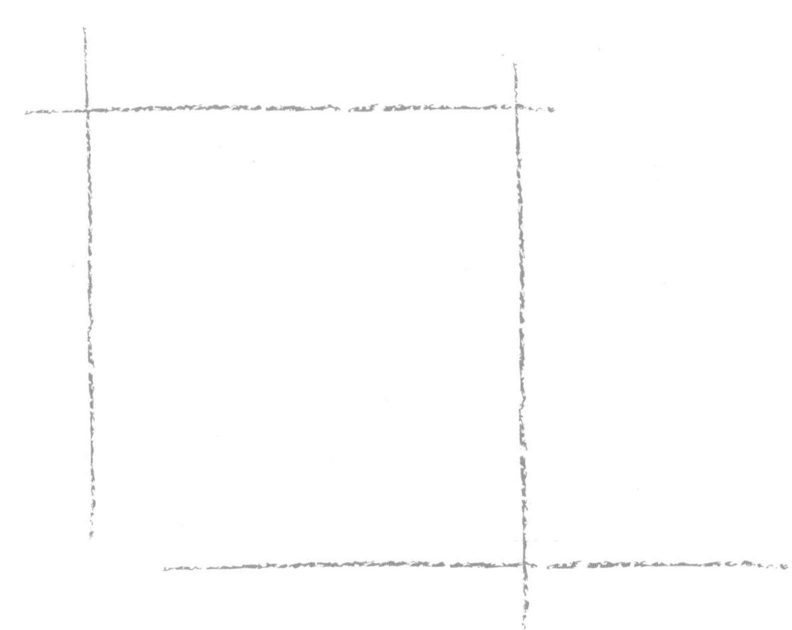

THE SENTINEL

This is one of the largest formations in the park, with an easy approach and great climbing. The nature trail takes you very close to the east face.

Finding the crag: Walk the Hidden Valley Nature Trail for about 300 feet to the nature trail's loop junction. The Sentinel can easily be seen as the large formation to the west with a tree near its summit. Take the left branch of the loop and walk about 400 feet. The Sentinel is the large formation to your left, just off the trail. To get to *Illusion Dweller,* continue on the nature trail past the north end of the rock, then cut left and around to the west face. Walk about 400 feet down along the west face into a narrow canyon; *Illusion Dweller* will be on your left. GPS coordinates are included with individual cliff descriptions.

Descent: Scramble (3rd class) down off the left (south) shoulder.

The Sentinel—East Face

This tall face receives morning sun and afternoon shade. Crag GPS: N34° 00.821'/W116° 10.264'

1. Ball Bearing (5.10a) **Pitch 1:** Climb a vertical crack, hand traverse right, jam a hand to finger crack, then make a final crux move up to a belay ledge with two bolts (100 feet). **Pitch 2:** Move right, then back left on a ramp to a vertical crack, which is followed to the top. **Pro:** to 3 inches, including two each from .75 to 2 inches.

2. Fote Hog (5.7 PG) **Pitch 1:** Climb a ramp up and left to a small tree. Face climb up about 20 feet with sparse protection, then traverse right for about 15 feet and power over a bulge on patina plates up to a belay ledge. **Pitch 2:** Climb a flake with a finger crack, then lieback a classic left-facing dihedral. Easier climbing takes you to the top. **Pro:** to 3 inches.

3. Look Ma, No Bolts (5.7 R) **Pitch 1:** Climb the initial ramp of *Fote Hog,* then move straight up the steep face (5.6 R) for about 30 feet. Climb out the left side of a small overhang, then face climb up and slightly right, over a steep bulge with plates up to a nice belay ledge at a small pine tree. **Pitch 2:** Easier (5.3) climbing leads up and left to the top. Belay from a large tree. **Pro:** .4 to 3 inches; bring a double runner to tie off a large plate.

The Sentinel—East Face

The Sentinel—West Face

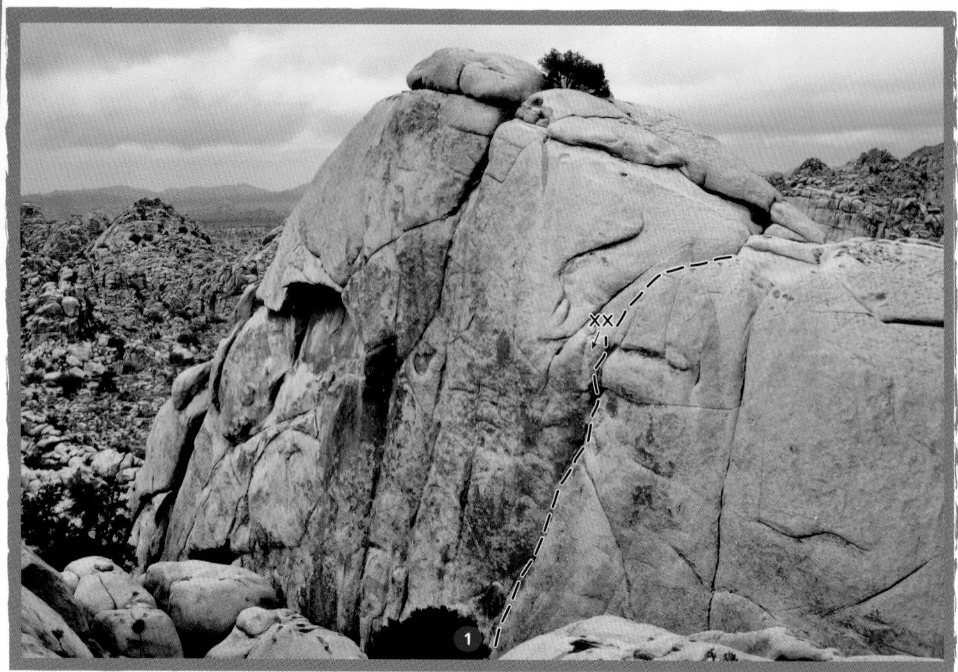

The Sentinel—West Face

This is one of the tallest vertical faces in Joshua Tree. It is in the shade in the morning and the sun in the afternoon. Crag GPS: N34° 00.841′/ W116° 10.436′

1. Illusion Dweller (5.10b) A popular crack climb up the obvious, right-leaning crack on the right side of the face. Jam a finger crack (5.9) to sustained hand and foot jamming, then power through the crux bulge. 2-bolt belay/rappel anchor. **Descent:** With a 60-meter rope you can just make it down, but the ends will be off the ground (100 feet-plus!) A 70-meter rope (or two ropes) is best. You can also climb a short pitch up an easy, wide crack to the top. Walk down slabs to the right, then head left back to the nature trail and follow it to the approach trail back around to the base.

Erik Kramer-Webb jamming on the classic crack *Illusion Dweller* (5.10b), The Sentinel.

Locomotion Rock

LOCOMOTION ROCK

This small cliff faces southwest and gets morning shade and afternoon sun.

Finding the crag: Walk the Hidden Valley Nature trail for several hundred feet to the nature trail's loop junction. Take the right branch of the loop and walk about 100 feet, then cut right, off the nature trail, on a marked climber's trail that leads directly to the rock. Crag GPS: N34° 00.802' / W116° 10.083'

Descent: Rappel 60 feet from bolts.

1. Leaping Leaner (5.6 PG) A classic moderate hand crack. The easiest start is to walk down into the pit and ascend the left side of the chockstone that leans against the wall. Another option is to do a committing step-across (unprotected) from the top of the chockstone. Once on the face, place pro in a shallow crack, traverse right on friction to reach the main crack, then jam your way to the top, where you'll find a 2-bolt anchor. You can also do a direct start from down in the pit to the right, jamming a shallow, right-leaning crack (5.9). **Pro:** to 3 inches.

SPORTS CHALLENGE ROCK

Steep climbing and excellent-quality rock characterize this formation. The east face is slightly overhanging and gets morning sun and afternoon shade. The vertical west face is in the shade in the morning and the sun in the afternoon.

Finding the crag: Hike the Hidden Valley Nature Trail for about 300 feet to the nature trail's loop junction. To reach the west face, take the right fork of the loop and walk about 100 feet. Turn left off the nature trail and walk directly to the west side. For the east face, turn right at the loop junction and walk right for about 300 feet. The east face will be on your left. *The trail loops around; it actually is about 300 ft.* Crag GPS: N34° 00.826' / W116° 10.130'

Descent: You can rappel from the bolt anchor on top of *Rap Bolters Are Weak* (less than 100 feet), or downclimb (4th or easy 5th class) the south shoulder.

Sports Challenge Rock—West Face

1. Sphincter Quits (5.10a PG) Jam a right-leaning crack to a block, then step right and climb a thin crack (5.10a) up to a ledge. Finish up the corner on the right. Gear anchor. **Pro:** thin to 3 inches.

2. What's It to You (5.10d PG) Traverse left across a horizontal crack to a vertical thin crack. You can clip the first bolt on *Rap Bolters Are Weak* to protect the traverse. Join *Sphincter Quits* to the top. **Pro:** to 3 inches.

3. Rap Bolters Are Weak (5.12a) Sport. Crimp your way up the steep patina face past five bolts to a 2-bolt belay/rappel anchor. Beware, some of the flakes are a bit flexy.

Sports Challenge Rock—West Face

Sports Challenge Rock—East Face

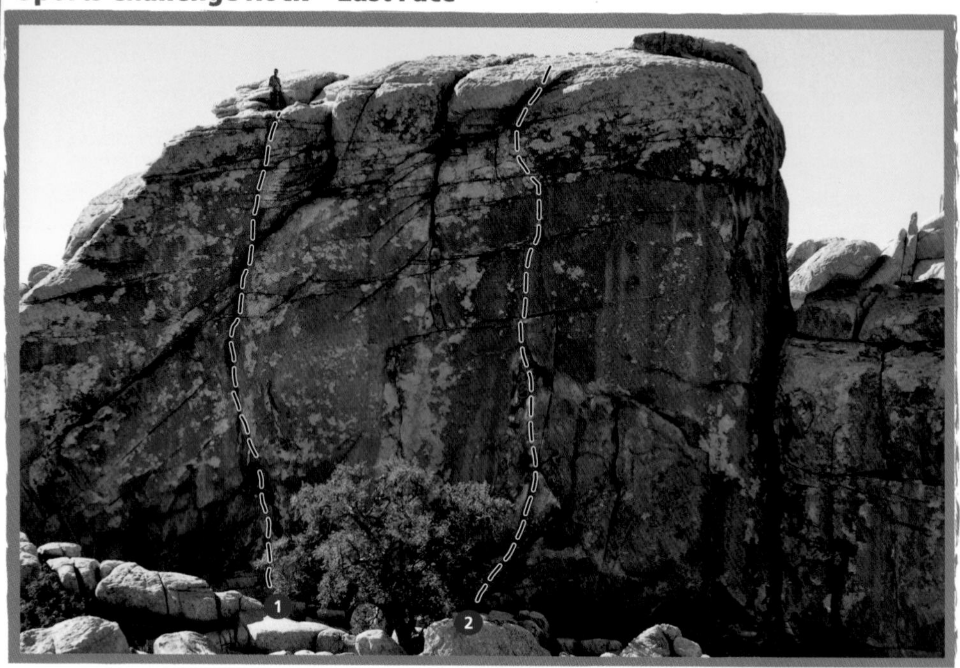

Sports Challenge Rock—East Face

1. Clean and Jerk (5.11a) Crank a bouldery start (5.11-), then jam a vertical, slightly overhanging crack. Gear anchor. **Pro:** to 3 inches.

2. Leave It to Beaver (5.12a) A classic testpiece with fantastic moves on excellent rock. Usually toproped, but the pro is good for leading. Gear anchor. **Pro:** .4 to 3 inches.

Leave It to Beaver was one of the first 5.12 climbs done in the park. The legendary John Bachar toproped the first free ascent in 1978 and did the first lead of the route in 1979. He would later go on to make many free solo ascents of the route.

Hidden Tower

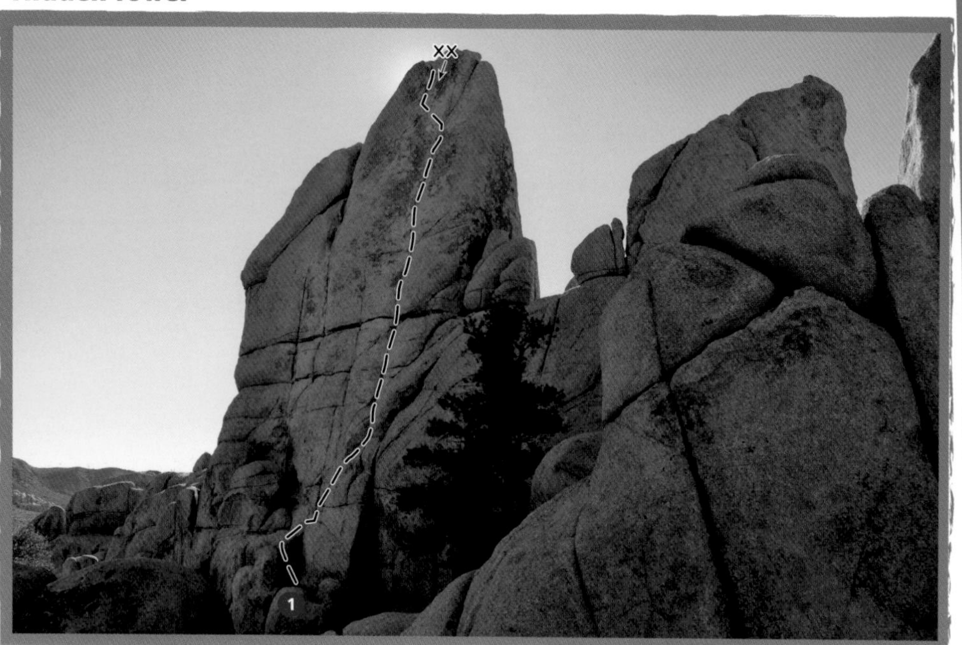

HIDDEN TOWER

This small tower has one of Joshua Tree's most popular 5.8 routes. It is in the sun in the morning, then the shade for the rest of the day. In the winter this face gets no sun.

Finding the crag: Hike the Hidden Valley Nature Trail for about 300 feet to the nature trail's loop junction. Turn right at the loop junction and walk for about 300 feet, until the east face of Sports Challenge Rock can be seen to your left. Turn right off the nature trail and you'll see the Hidden Tower directly ahead. The trail leads around the left side of the tower to the base of the northeast face. Crag GPS: N34° 00.880' / W116° 10.096'

Descent: Rappel 80 feet from the bolt anchor.

1. Sail Away (5.8) Fun climbing with good protection up a vertical crack. Where the crack thins near the top, you can reach left and finish up a flake. 2-bolt belay/rappel anchor. **Pro:** to 2 inches.

Annelen Kahl leading *Sail Away* (5.8) on the Hidden Tower. Photo Greg Epperson

HOUSER BUTTRESS

This large buttress faces south and is very sheltered from north winds. The cliff is in the sun most of the day—a good choice on cold days.

Finding the crag: From the Real Hidden Valley parking area, walk west on a marked climber's trail for about 200 yards. You'll see Houser Buttress on the right. A bit of 3rd-class scrambling leads to the base. Crag GPS: N34° 00.624' / W116° 10.269'

1. Loose Lady (5.10a PG) Climb the left side of the impressive buttress past seven bolts. The climbing is sustained and a bit runout. 2-bolt belay/rappel anchor. **Descent:** Rappel 100 feet from the bolt anchor. With a 70-meter rope you can lower off from the anchor to the big, flat ledge at the base.

2. Lady Fingers (5.10b) **Pitch 1:** Climb a short, easy (5.0) pitch up to a belay at a chockstone (3-inch cam). **Pitch 2:** Nice edging past five bolts leads up to a gear belay (0.5 to 3 inches). **Descent:** Rappel down *Lucky Lady*.

3. Lucky Lady (5.8 PG) A good warm-up, both physically and psychologically, for *Loose Lady*. Friction and mantles lead past two bolts to a 2-bolt belay/rappel anchor (less than 100 feet). **Pro:** a 1.5-inch cam for the start.

Houser Buttress

Echo Rock Area

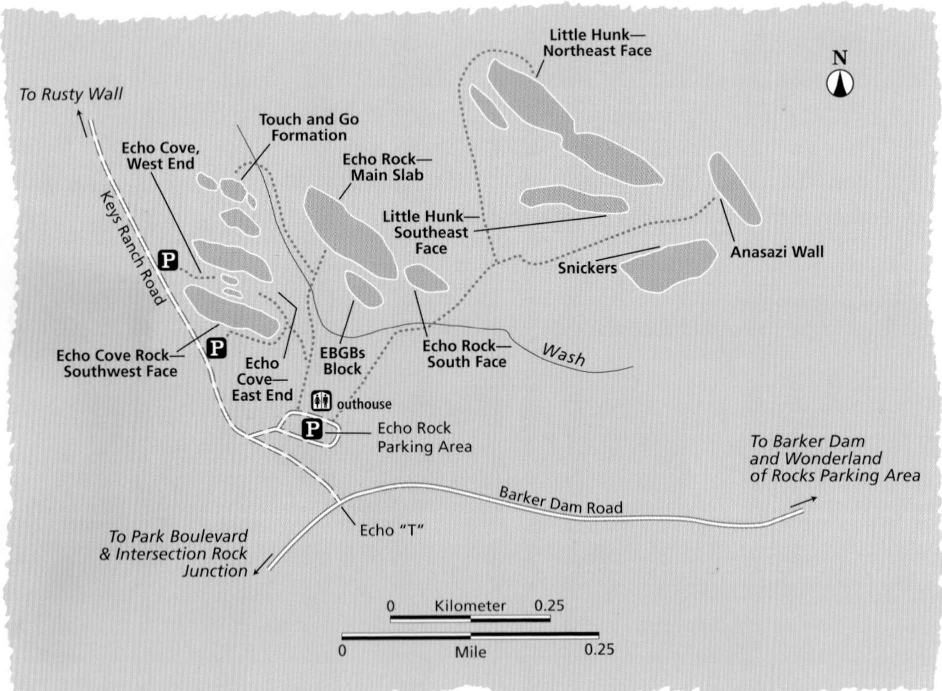
Little Hunk—
Northeast Face
N
To Rusty Wall
Touch and Go
Formation
Echo Cove,
West End
Echo Rock—
Main Slab
Keys Ranch Road
Little Hunk—
Southeast
Face
Anasazi Wall
Snickers
P
P
Echo Cove Rock—
Southwest Face
Echo
Cove—
East End
EBGBs
Block
Echo Rock—
South Face
Wash
outhouse
P
Echo Rock
Parking Area
To Barker Dam
and Wonderland
of Rocks Parking Area
Barker Dam Road
Echo "T"
To Park Boulevard
& Intersection Rock
Junction
0 Kilometer 0.25
0 Mile 0.25

7. Echo Rock Area

This popular area represents what makes climbing at Joshua Tree so special: easy approaches to a remarkable diversity of splendid slab, face, and crack climbs with a choice of sunny or shady cliffs.

Getting there: From the Intersection Rock Junction, drive 0.1 mile south and turn left at the Barker Dam/ Keys Ranch Road. Drive east for 0.6 mile, then turn left at the fork (called the Echo "T") onto the dirt Keys Ranch Road. Go 0.1 mile and turn right to enter the large Echo Rock parking area (GPS: N34° 01.367' / W116° 09.415'). There is an outhouse and marked climber's access trails. Echo Cove—West End parking is 0.3 mile north from the Echo T, and the Rusty Wall parking area is 1 mile north of the Echo T.

ECHO COVE ROCK—SOUTHWEST FACE

Finding the crag: From the Echo Rock parking area, this face is clearly visible about 200 yards to the northwest. A marked climber's trail leads to the rock. You can also park very close to the rock at a small parking area 0.2 mile north of the Echo T. Crag GPS: N34° 01.455' / W116° 09.480'

Descent: Rappel from bolts (less than 100 feet) at the top of *RML*.

Echo Cove Rock—Southwest Face Overview

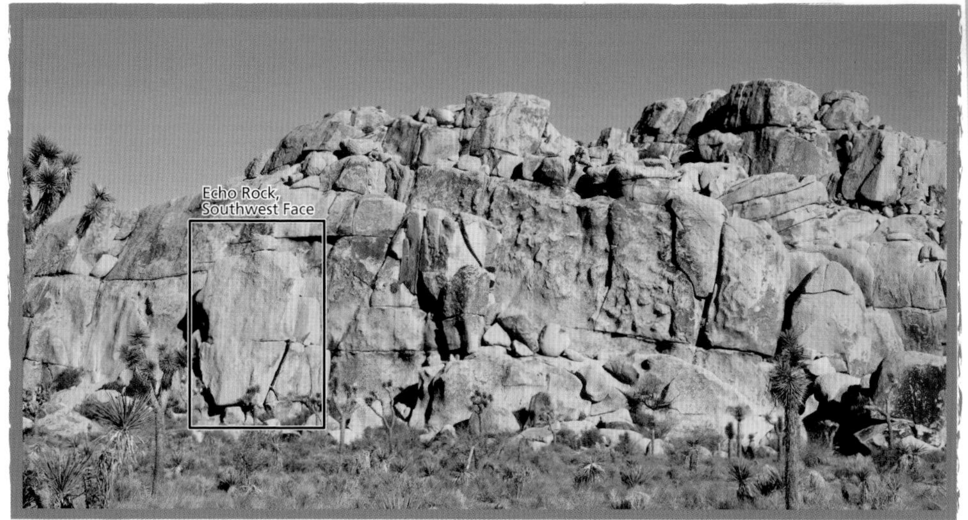

Echo Cove Rock—Southwest Face

1. RML (5.9) Power over an overhang to a tricky mantle (crux), then step left and climb a friction slab with three bolts. 2-bolt belay/rappel anchor. **Pro:** a few pieces for the start.

2. CS Special (5.10b PG/R) Crank (5.10-, bad landing) over a small roof, then climb a steep slab (5.10b) past four bolts up to the top. Gear anchor (thread). **Descent:** Rappel RML.

ECHO COVE—WEST END

This side of Echo Cove is very popular because of its wide range of high-quality routes and easy access. The left side faces southwest, receives sun all day long, and is sheltered from north winds, making it a good choice for cold winter days. The right side has steep face climbing on excellent, featured rock. It faces northeast and is in the shade most of the time, making it a good choice for warmer days.

Finding the crag: From the Intersection Rock Junction, drive 0.1 mile south and turn left at the Barker Dam/Keys Ranch Road. Drive east for 0.6 mile, then turn left at the fork (called the Echo "T") onto the dirt Keys Ranch Road). Go 0.3 mile and turn right into a small parking area. The southwest face is on the left and the northeast face is on the right as you walk into the cove. Crag GPS: N34° 01.507'/W116° 09.549'

1. Fun Stuff (5.8/9 PG) Start with a thin move right off the ground (5.9-), then face climb (5.8 PG) to a bolt about 30 feet up. A better protected variation is 20 feet left, up to and over a slight bulge (5.9) past a bolt. Face climb (5.7) up to a right-leaning dihedral, with an exciting move to exit and gain the top. 2-bolt belay/rappel anchor. **Descent:** Rappel 80 feet from bolt anchor. **Pro:** to 3 inches.

Echo Cove—West End, Southwest Face, Left Side

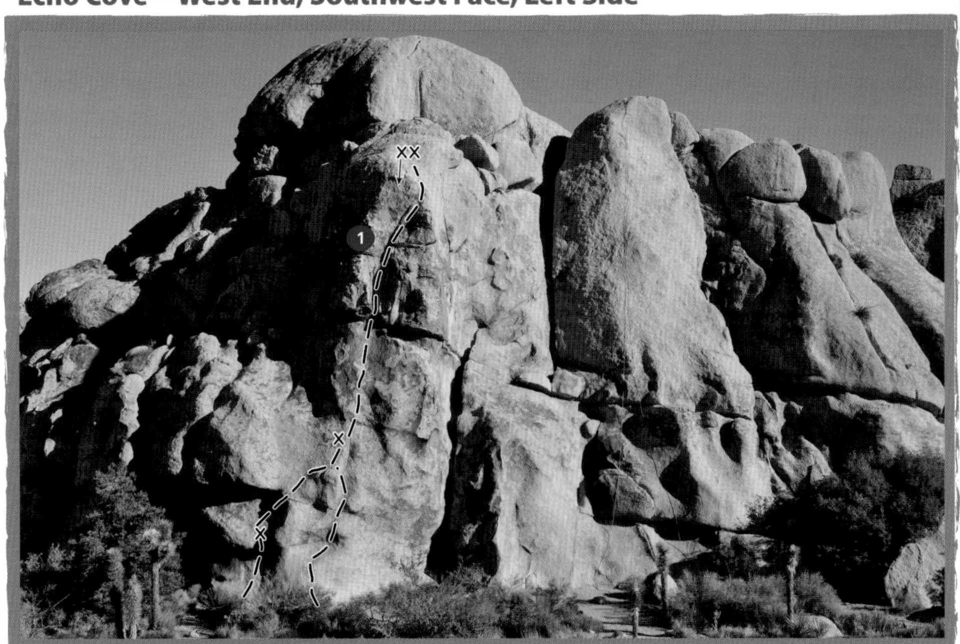

Echo Cove—West End, Southwest Face, Right Side

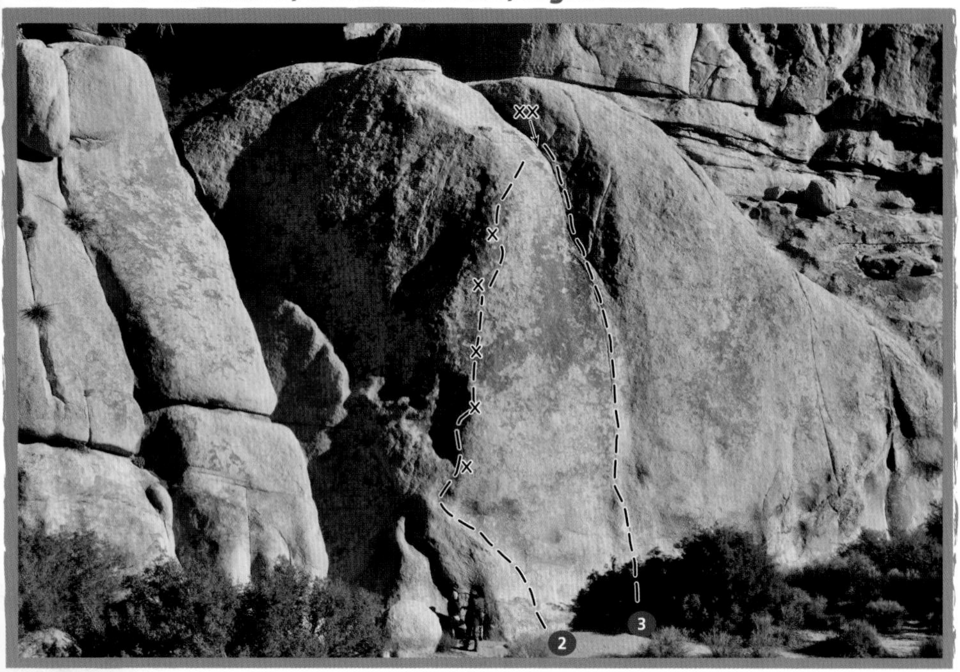

2. Swing Low (5.7+/5.8-) Sport. Superb friction climbing past five bolts up to a 2-bolt belay/rappel anchor. The crux is moving past a brief lieback flake at the last bolt. **Descent:** Rappel from bolt anchor (less than 100 feet).

3. Pinky Lee (5.10d/11a PG/R) Climb a thin slab up to a steep, thin crack. Easily toproped off the *Swing Low* anchor. **Pro:** to 2 inches.

Echo Cove—West End, Northeast Face

4. Ground Up or Shut Up (5.11b) Quality face climbing past six bolts on the steep face just left of *Boulderdash*. 2-bolt lower-off anchor. **Pro:** optional medium cam before the fourth bolt.

5. Boulderdash (5.9+ PG) Face climb up to a classic, slightly overhanging dihedral. Easily toproped by scrambling up the right shoulder and rigging a gear anchor (.5 to 3 inches). The start is bouldery, and easier with a cheater stone. **Descent:** Scramble (3rd class) down to slabs on the right shoulder (toward the road).

6. Big Moe (5.11a/b R/X) A popular toprope with excellent, overhanging face moves on high-quality rock. The initial section has a reachy crux (or dyno), and the final section will get your forearms pumping. 2-bolt anchor on top. **Descent:** Scramble (3rd class) down the slabs/right shoulder of the face.

Rusty Wall

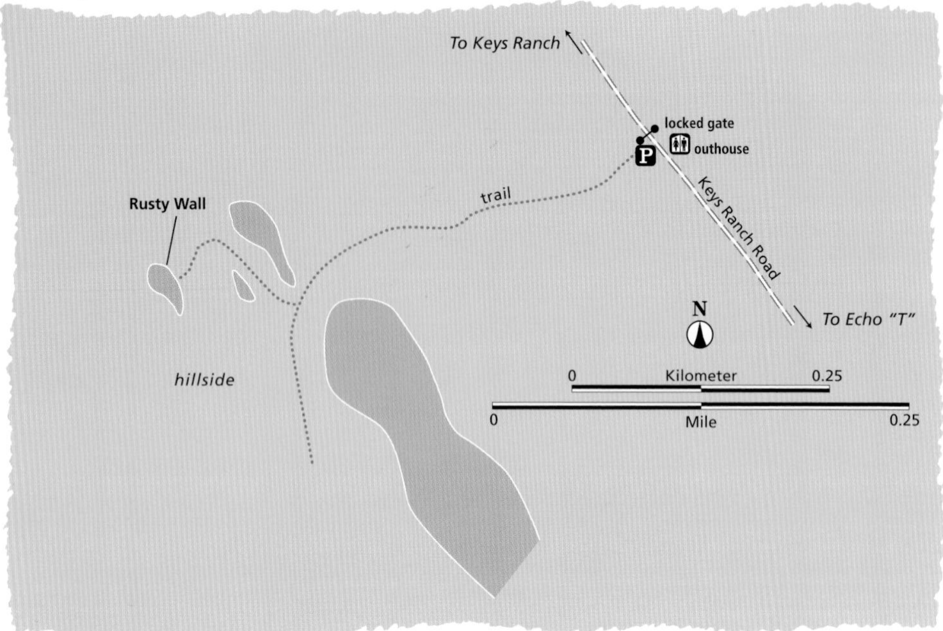

RUSTY WALL

This slightly overhanging cliff of beautiful orange granite features two of Joshua Tree's best crack climbs. It faces northeast and is in the sun in the morning, then in the shade in the afternoon. It gets very little sun in the winter months.

Getting there: From the Intersection Rock Junction, drive 0.1 mile south and turn left at the Barker Dam/ Keys Ranch Road. Drive east for 0.6 mile, then turn left at the fork (called the Echo "T") onto the dirt Keys Ranch Road. Go 1 mile and park at a small parking area with an outhouse and a locked gate (the Keys Ranch Tours meet here). You can see the Rusty Wall from the parking area, about 400 yards to the west. A well-defined trail leads up to the crag with a bit of scrambling (3rd class) up to the base. Crag GPS: N34° 02.010' / W116° 10.020'

Descent: You can easily scramble up the left (4th class) or right (3rd class) side of the crag to access or descend from the top.

Rusty Wall

1. Wangerbanger (5.11c) This is the left crack, with great jams up to a strenuous pod. Gear anchor (.75 to 3 inches). **Pro:** double set of cams to 3 inches.

2. O'Kelleys Crack (5.11a/b) A hard start (5.11-, try a fist jam, palm out) leads to 5.10 jamming with a little bit of everything: fingers, hands, liebacking, and some off-width. Gear anchor (1.75 to 2 inches). **Pro:** to 4 inches.

Claret cup cactus flowers bloom in late spring and early summer.

Echo Cove—East End Overview

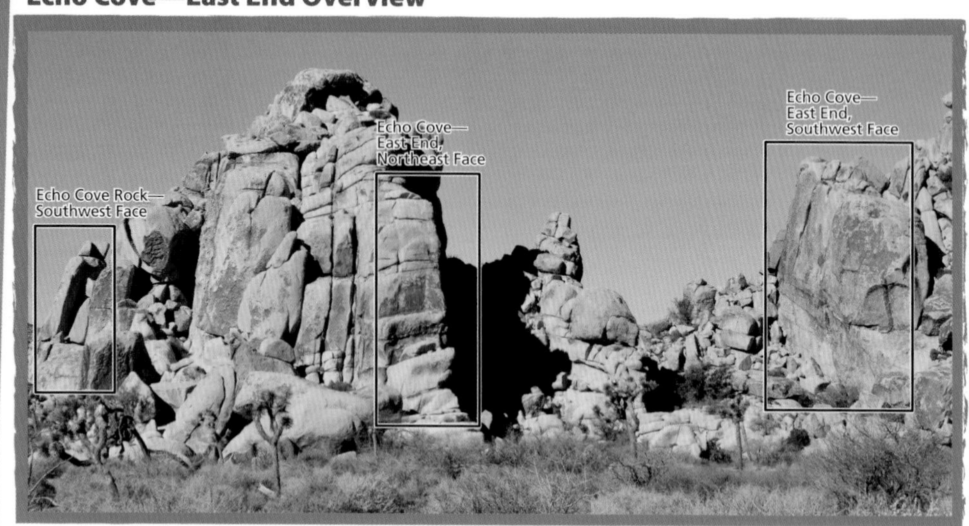

ECHO COVE—EAST END

Echo Cove—East End, Northeast Face

Finding the crag: From the Echo Rock parking area, walk north for about 100 yards on a marked climber's trail to reach the east end of Echo Cove. The northeast face is on the left side as you walk into the cove's east end. It is in the sun in the early morning, then in the shade all day. In the winter it gets very little sun. Crag GPS: N34° 01.469' / W116° 09.444'

Descent: 4th class. Look for a deep chimney capped with a 3 foot diameter chockstone about 40 feet down the opposite (southwest) side, directly behind *Halfway to Paradise* and *Effigy Too.* Chimney down through the chasm, then scramble back around to the base.

1. Hatfield Arête (5.8) Stem across to jam a gritty crack, then climb the face left of the arête past three bolts. Gear anchor. **Pro:** to 3 inches.

2. Hatfields and McCoys (5.10c to 5.11a) Stem across to jam a gritty crack, then step right and climb a steep face with excellent rock past three bolts to the top. At the third bolt it's easier (5.10c) moving left to the arête, harder (5.11-) going straight up. Gear anchor. **Pro:** .4 to 4 inches.

3. Halfway to Paradise (5.10b PG/R) Climb the steep face on excellent rock past one bolt (crux), then move up and right to finish up a short crack. Gear anchor. **Pro:** thin to 2.5 inches. A 40-foot length of static rope is useful to encircle a solid block of rock for a toprope anchor.

4. Effigy Too (5.10b PG) The crux is the first 15 feet: bouldery and hard to protect. After that the crack is about 5.8, with good protection. Gear anchor. **Pro:** to 3 inches.

5. Misfits (5.11b) A hidden gem. Start about 50 feet right of *Effigy Too,* below a large boulder. Climb a thin crack up to a right-leaning corner, then up a steep face to the top. **Descent:** Two bolts on top, but they're not set up for rappelling, so do the downclimb. **Pro:** three bolts, gear to 2.5 inches.

Echo Cove—East End, Northeast Face

Echo Cove—East End, Southwest Face

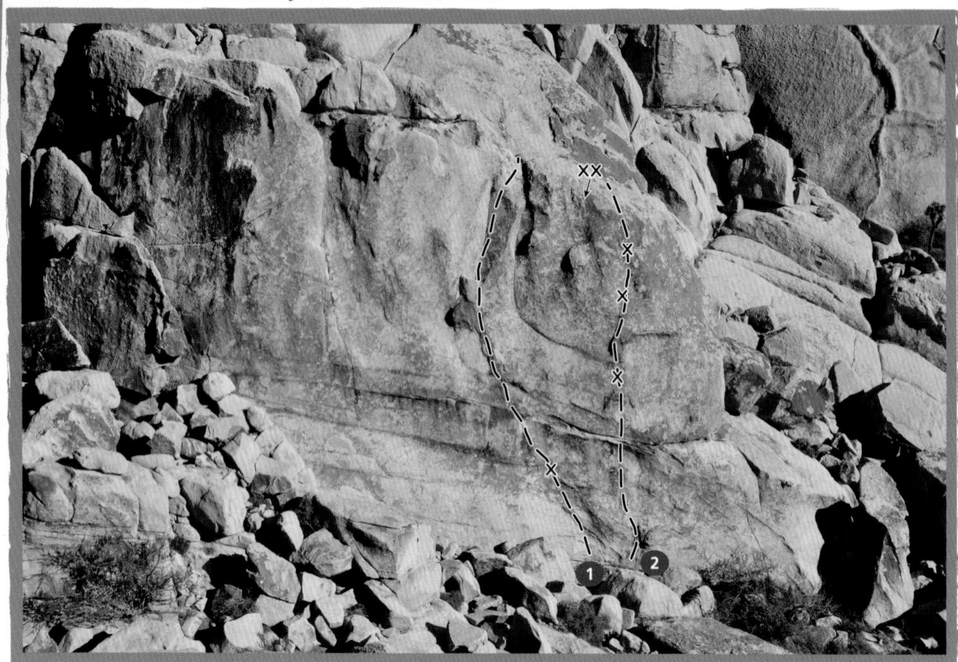

Echo Cove—East End, Southwest Face

Finding the crag: From the Echo Rock parking area, walk north for about 100 yards on a marked climber's trail to reach the east end of Echo Cove. The southwest face is on the right side as you walk into the cove's east end. It is in the sun most of the day and is sheltered from north and west winds: a good spot for a cold day. Crag GPS: N34° 01.543' / W116° 09.440'

Descent: Scramble off to the right, or rappel from the *Solo Dog* anchor bolts.

1. No Mistake or Big Pancake (5.11a) Face climb past a bolt to a left-leaning thin crack system that leads to the top. Gear anchor. **Pro:** thin to 2.5 inches.

2. Solo Dog (5.11b) Start 10 feet right of *No Mistake or Big Pancake*. Face climb up seams to a horizontal crack, then up the face past three bolts to the top. 2-bolt belay/rappel anchor. **Pro:** to 1 inch, including some very thin nuts.

Tony Sartin leading *Solo Dog* (5.11b) at Echo Cove. PHOTO GREG EPPERSON

Echo Rock—Main Slab Overview

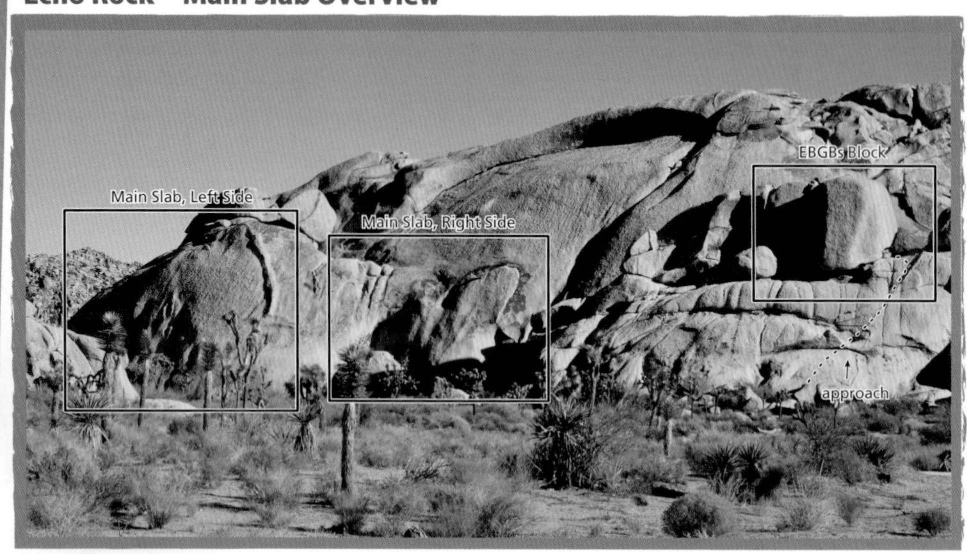

ECHO ROCK—MAIN SLAB

This huge slab gets shade in the early morning, then sun all day—a good choice for cooler conditions.

Finding the crag: From the Echo Rock parking area, follow a marked climber's trail for about 200 yards north to the rock. Crag GPS: N34° 01.520' / W116° 09.396'

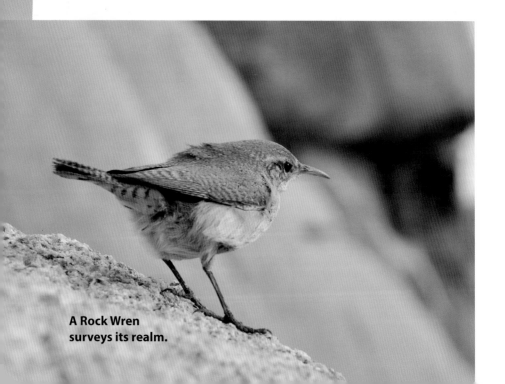

A Rock Wren surveys its realm.

Echo Rock—Main Slab, Left Side

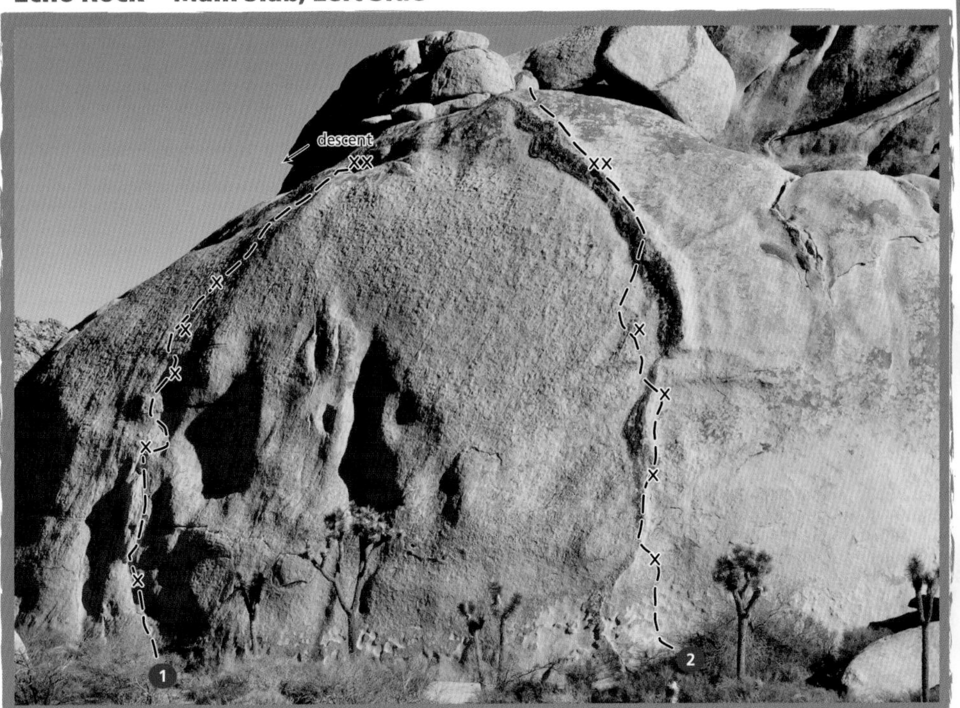

1. Double Dip (5.6 PG) Climb the slab past one bolt to reach a huge lieback flake (3- to 4-inch cams). From the top of the flake, stretch up to clip a bolt, then step right onto a slab and climb up to a steeper headwall (easiest on the left). Wind past three more bolts to the top 2-bolt belay/rappel anchor. **Descent:** Rappel 165 feet with two ropes, or walk off (3rd class) to the left (north). You can also traverse across the top (3rd class) about 200 feet to the right and rap *Forbidden Paradise* (80 feet).

2. Stichter Quits (5.8) An old Joshua classic that gets a little more polished and slippery every year. Climb up to and follow the huge brown dike (originally named *Black Tide*) past four bolts to a 2-bolt belay/rappel anchor. Rappel from here with two ropes or a 70-meter rope (113 feet), or continue up a short 4th-class pitch to the top. Gear anchor. **Descent:** Walk off to the left (north) via 3rd-class slabs, or go about 100 feet to the right and rap *Forbidden Paradise* (80 feet).

Echo Rock—Main Slab, Right Side

3. Forbidden Paradise (5.10b) Sustained thin-hold slab climbing past six bolts to a 2-bolt belay/rappel anchor (80 feet). Much easier on a cool day! **Pro:** You can place an optional nut or small cam between the first and second bolts.

4. Heart and Sole (5.10a/b PG) A little scary to the first bolt, although you can place a thin cam in a hollow flake for psychological protection. Climb up and right (5.10-) to a second bolt, then tiptoe left across the lip of the roof (5.10-) past a third bolt, moving left to reach a right-facing dihedral. Lieback this to the top. 3-bolt belay/rappel anchor (80 feet). **Pro:** to 2.5 inches.

ECHO ROCK—EBGBs BLOCK

This famous block has one of Joshua Tree's classic face climbs—EBGBs, notorious for its difficult mantle onto the face, then hair raising, runnout slab climbing above. Best done during cooler conditions for optimal friction.

Finding the crag: From the Echo Rock parking area, the EBGBs block can clearly be seen as the gigantic boulder perched high on the right side of Echo Rock's immense southwest face. Approach directly from the base, up a slab, underneath an arch, then up a dike to the start (4th class). Crag GPS: N34° 01.457' / W116° 09.350'

> In 1985 a climber fell off the last moves of *EBGBs* and sheared the original homemade aluminum bolt hanger placed on the first ascent, taking a 40-foot plunge. He survived with only a broken ankle. Subsequently, all the bolts have been replaced.

1. EBGBs (5.10d) Start with a tough mantle, then climb a steep slab with an exciting runout (5.8) at the top. To better belay your second on the mantleshelf, a good strategy is to pull the rope, then toss it back down. 5 bolts to a 2-bolt anchor. **Descent:** The rappel bolts are on the south side.

Echo Rock—EBGBs Block

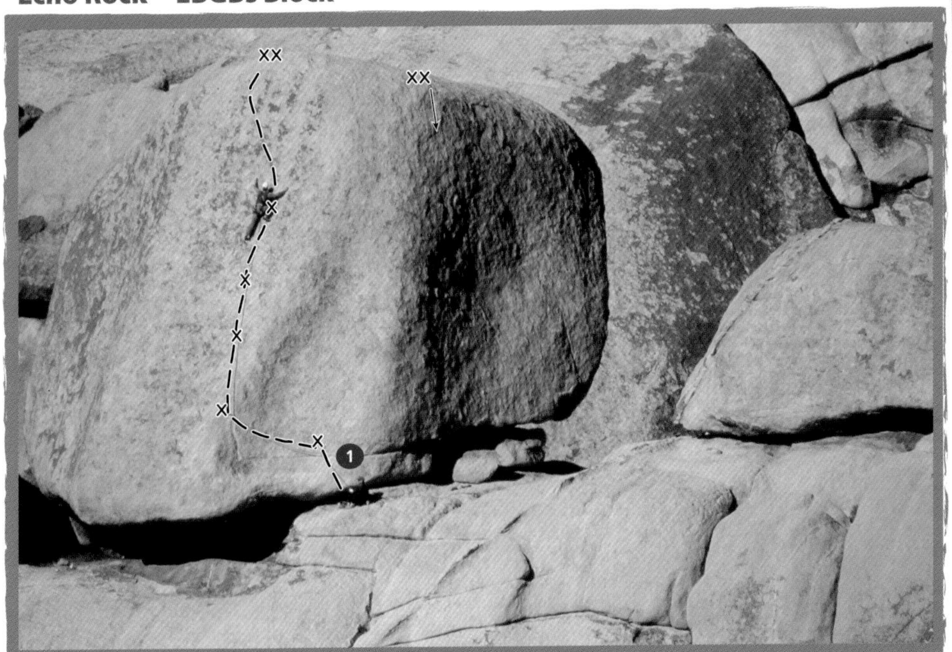

Touch and Go Formation

TOUCH AND GO FORMATION

This crag has one of Joshua Tree's classic 5.9 dihedrals. It faces north and is in the sun in the early morning, then the shade all day.

Finding the crag: From the Echo Rock parking lot, follow the marked climber's trail into the wash about 200 feet past the Echo Rock—Main Slab, Left Side area. Touch and Go is the high cliff on the left, facing Echo Rock's main slab. Crag GPS: N34° 01.543' / W116° 09.440'

1. Touch and Go (5.9) Climb the crack in a beautiful corner. The only bummer about this route is that it isn't longer! Gear anchor. **Descent:** Downclimb (4th class) on the opposite (left) side. **Pro:** to 3 inches.

Echo Rock—South Face Overview

ECHO ROCK—SOUTH FACE

This sunny, immense, south-facing wall is very sheltered, and a good choice for cold, windy days. *Swept Away* is in the shade in the early morning.

Finding the crag: From the Echo Rock parking area, follow a marked climber's trail that leads northeast for about 300 yards to the formation. Crag GPS: N34° 01.447' / W116° 09.302'

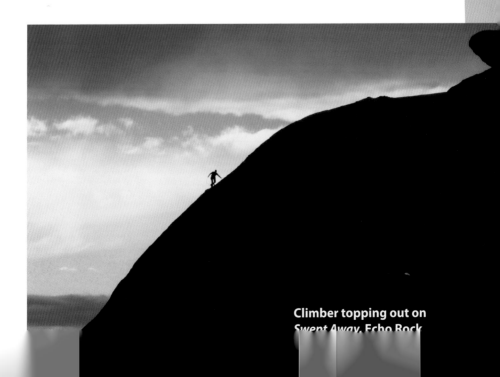

Climber topping out on *Swept Away*, Echo Rock

Echo Rock—South Face, Left Side

1. Pope's Crack (5.9 or 5.10b) Jam the sustained vertical crack to where the angle lessens, then you have three choices: **Standard finish:** Traverse left about 20 feet across a dike on a slab, then up a vertical crack to the top. Gear anchor (1 to 3 inches). **Direct finish (5.10b):** Continue straight up the big roof, clip a fixed pin, then make a move up to a bolt. Reach right from the bolt (5.10b), then up an easy slab to the top. Gear anchor (1 to 3 inches). **Right finish:** Move right to a dike (5.7) and belay about 30 feet higher. Gear anchor (1 to 2 inches). **Descent:** Climb down the slab to the right (exposed, 4th class) and rappel 80 feet from bolts. **Pro:** to 3 inches, including many from 1.5 to 2.5 inches.

Echo Rock—South Face, Right Side

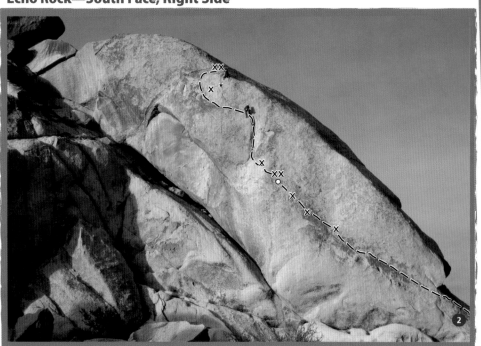

2. Swept Away (5.11a) This 2-pitch classic climbs the imposing face of the huge, sweeping buttress on the far right side of the south face. **Pitch 1:** Climb around the left side of a corner, then go diagonally left along a ramp and straight up past three bolts (5.10a) to a 2-bolt hanging belay. **Pitch 2:** (5.11a) Face climb left past a bolt to reach a corner (crux). Follow the corner to easier climbing up and left to a bolt, then move right across a dike to a 2-bolt belay/rappel anchor (80 feet). **Pro:** to 2 inches.

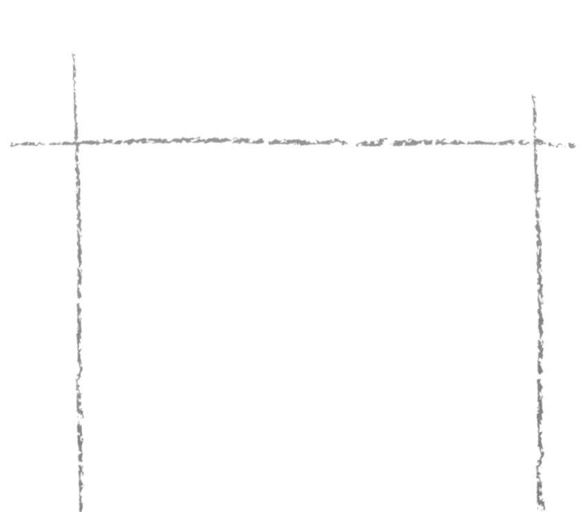

Snickers/Little Hunk/Anasazi Wall Overview

SNICKERS

This tall cliff faces north and is very shaded most of the time, so it's a good choice during warmer weather. In late spring it stays in the shade until about 2 p.m.

Finding the crag: From the Echo Rock parking area, walk northeast on a marked climber's trail around the right (south) side of the main Echo Rock formation, then continue northeast for about 250 yards into a canyon. The north face of Snickers will be on your right, well into the canyon. Crag GPS: N34° 01.521'/ W116° 09.034'

1. Norwegian Wood (5.9) Jam and stem your way up the corner. At the top the crack widens to fist size. A few larger cams are needed for the top section and a gear anchor. **Descent:** Rappel 100 feet from bolts about 30 feet to the right. **Pro:** some thin nuts, cams from .4 to 4.5 inches.

2. Joyride (5.11c) Start just right of *Norwegian Wood* and climb the face past eight bolts to a 2-bolt lower-off anchor (100 feet). The tough parts are a thin slab section at the second bolt (crux) and a 5.11- move to get to the anchor. **Pro:** Bring some cams from .5 to .75 inches to supplement the bolt protection.

3. Funny Bone (5.8-) A fun variety of face climbing moves that follows a crack system. At the top, move right to a 2-bolt belay/rappel anchor (80 feet). **Pro:** single rack to 3.5 inches.

4. Humorous (5.10b) Begin 15 feet right of *Funny Bone* with a mantle on a horizontal crack. Climb a steep face past two bolts (5.10b), then climb a slightly overhanging section (5.10a) past two more bolts up to a ledge with a 2-bolt belay/rappel anchor (80 feet). **Pro:** Bring a few nuts and tiny cams to supplement the bolts. The *Ridiculous Finish* (5.11b) extends the pitch above the anchor past two more bolts to a higher anchor (100 feet).

5. Crime of the Century (5.11a) Climb the crack through a roof to a ledge with a 2-bolt belay/rappel anchor (50 feet). **Pro:** to 3.5 inches.

Snickers

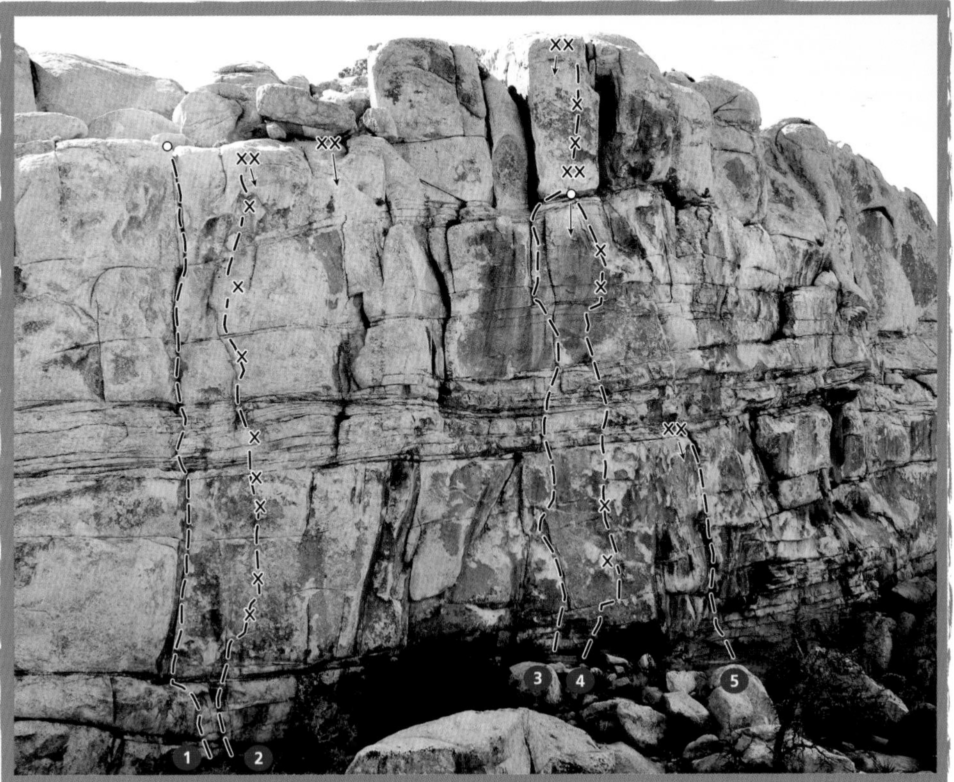

LITTLE HUNK—SOUTH FACE

A sunny, sheltered wall that is good for cooler weather.

Finding the crag: From the Echo Rock parking area, walk northeast on a marked climber's trail around the right (south) side of the main Echo Rock formation, then continue northeast for about 250 yards into a canyon. The south face of the Little Hunk will be on your left, well into the canyon. *The Paw* is around the corner on the far right side of the formation. Crag GPS: N34° 01.541' / W116° 09.024'

1. Right Between the Eyes (5.7) A fun and exciting traversing pitch. Start by walking left on a ledge to a cave-like belay area. Traverse left a few feet, then climb up about 20 feet to reach a horizontal crack. Hand traverse left for about 60 feet to a 2-bolt anchor. You can lower off from the anchor and belay from the ground to better watch your second. Take care to protect your follower. **Pro:** Bring at least a double set of cams from .5 to 3 inches (including three 2.5 inch cams).

On the first ascent of *Right Between the Eyes,* my wife, Yvonne, pulled off a large chunk of rock while following. I couldn't see her but heard a sharp scream. She assured me she was okay. When she got to the belay, she was bleeding from a small wound . . . right between the eyes.

Little Hunk—South Face

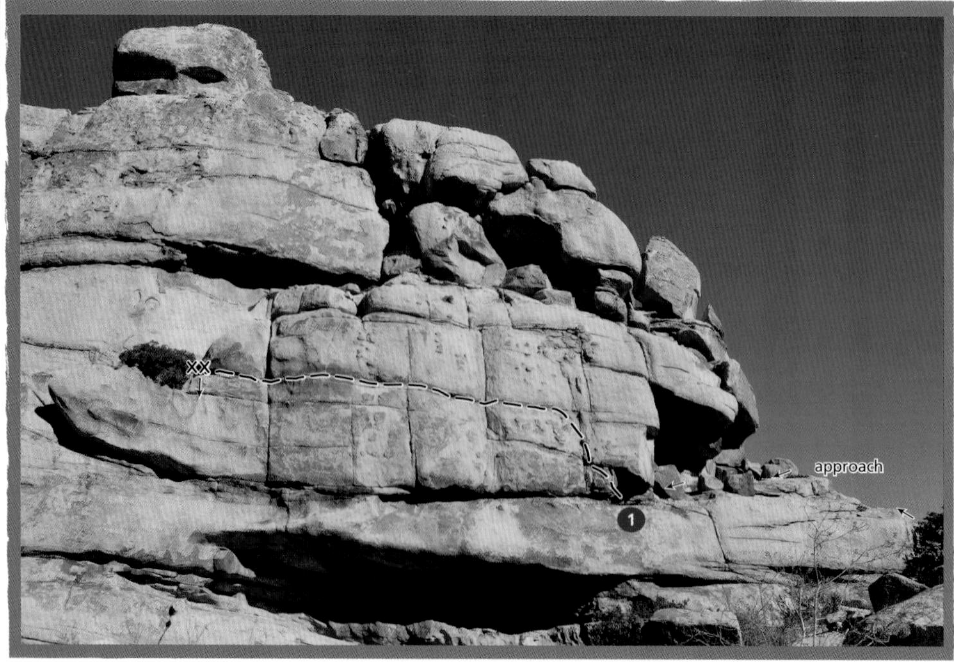

Little Hunk—Southeast Face

2. The Paw (5.10c) Sport. Located on the southeast face of Little Hunk. A very short and steep face climb on nice rock, with four bolts and one fixed pin to a 2-bolt lower-off anchor. This climb gets sun in the morning and shade in the afternoon. It's a good warm-up for *Physical Graffiti* on the Anasazi Wall. Route GPS: N34° 01.537' / W116° 08.999'

Anasazi Wall

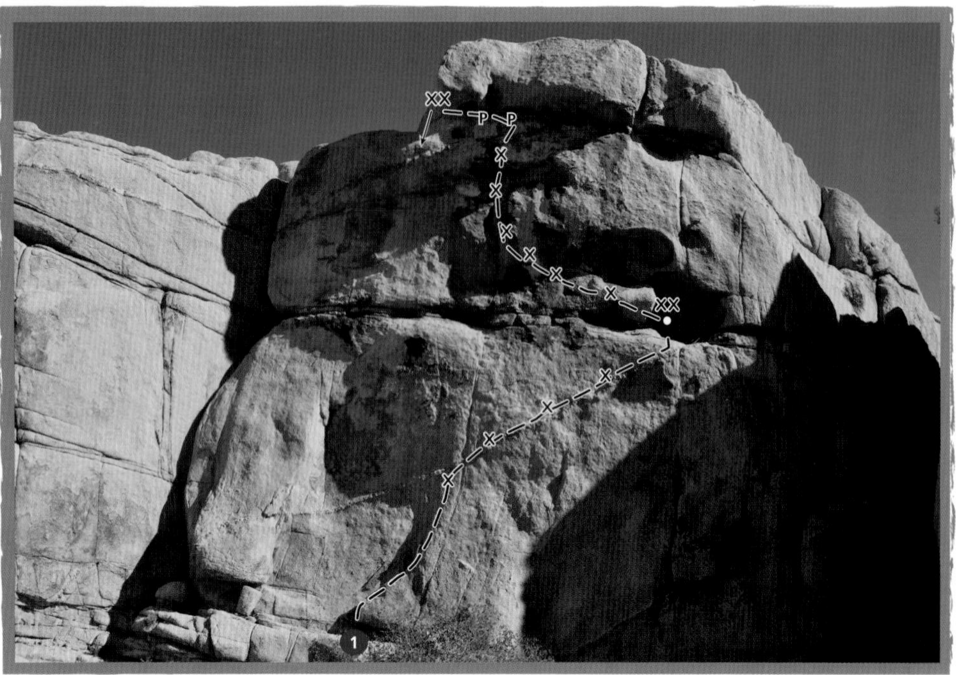

ANASAZI WALL

An alluring cliff with a unique sport climb. It faces west and gets shade in the early morning, then sun for the rest of the day.

Finding the crag: From the Echo Rock parking area, walk northeast on a marked climber's trail around the right (south) side of the main Echo Rock formation, then continue northeast for about 250 yards into a canyon. Walk through the canyon between the Snickers and Big Hunk formations; Anasazi Wall is 100 yards straight ahead. Crag GPS: N34° 01.572' / W166 08.916'

1. Physical Graffiti (5.11a) Sport. **Pitch 1:** Climb up to and hand traverse the dike past four bolts to a bolted belay in a cave. **Pitch 2:** (six bolts, two fixed pins) Traverse left, up a vertical crack, then over an overhang up to a horizontal crack. Traverse left to a bolt belay. **Descent:** Rappel 80 feet. Can be done in one pitch if you use long slings and go back and unclip a few bolts, but then you miss out on the cool cave belay!

LITTLE HUNK—NORTHEAST FACE

This face has a great collection of steep slab routes on excellent rock. It is in the sun in the morning and the shade in the afternoon. In late spring it doesn't get shade until about 2 p.m.

Finding the crag: From the Echo Rock parking area, follow the marked climber's trail northeast around the right (south) side of the main Echo Rock formation, then veer left (north), following a well-defined trail that leads several hundred yards to the left end of the massive west side of the Little Hunk formation. The northeast face is just around the corner to the right. Crag GPS: N34° 01.671' / W116° 09.169'

1. Changes (5.11c/d) Sport. Start from a gully on the far left side of the cliff. Climb an easy slab to a steep headwall with a technical crux (5.11+), then move left and climb a steep but easier face to the top. 9 bolts to a 2-bolt anchor. **Descent:** Rappel 100 feet from the bolts. To rig a toprope, bring a length of static rope, as the anchor is about 20 feet back from the edge.

2. Blues Traveler (5.10c/d) Sport. This is the first route immediately left of *ZZZZ*. 4 bolts to a 2-bolt anchor. **Descent:** Rappel 80 feet from the bolts.

Little Hunk—Northeast Face

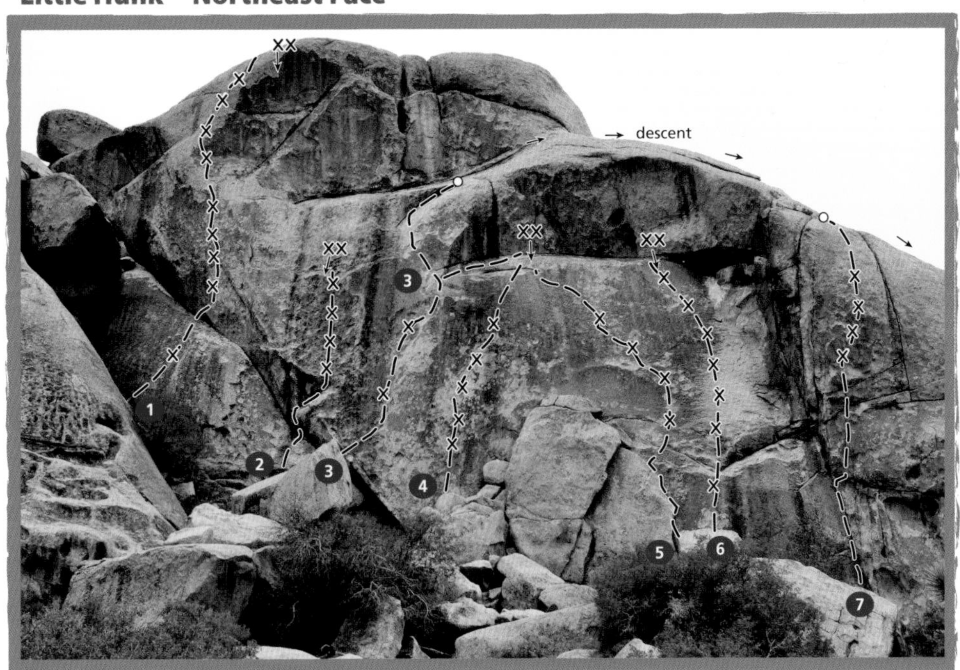

3. ZZZZ (5.9+ PG) Steep face climbing on beautiful rock with nice edges, but runout. You can place a 1.5-inch cam and use a sling on a horn before the first bolt. After the second bolt you can place a piece (1-inch cam) and move right to the *Electralux* bolt anchor (rap 80 feet), or climb up and left (the original line, 5.8 PG) and up to the top (gear anchor). **Descent:** Walk off (3rd class) down slabs to the right.

4. Electric Blue (5.11d) Sport. Climb a sustained face on edges to a crux pull onto a slab. 5 bolts to a 2-bolt belay/ rappel anchor shared with *Electralux* (80 feet). From this anchor you can also toprope *Blue Diamond* (5.10c), which is the route directly below the anchor.

5. Electralux (5.9) Scramble up to a ledge on the right, lieback a short flake, then prance up a slab with four bolts that lead up and left to a 2-bolt belay/rappel anchor (80 feet).

6. Incandescent (5.8) Sport. Begin just right of *Eletralux*. Make a height-dependent reach at the first bolt, then climb a well-protected, enjoyable slab past 6 more bolts to a 2-bolt belay/ rappel anchor (80 feet).

7. Power Failure (5.11a) Climb a crack (5.8/.9) for about 20 feet, then step right and face climb past seams to reach a slightly overhanging face with four bolts. You may have a power failure before you can unravel the tricky sequences. Gear anchor (3 to 4 inches). **Descent:** Walk off to the right (3rd class) down slabs. **Pro:** .4 to 1 inch.

8.

Wonderland of Rocks

The Wonderland of Rocks is a vast area of spectacular cliffs and domes in a pristine setting within the wilderness boundary of the park. Please practice Leave No Trace wilderness ethics if you climb here, and stay on climber's trails to minimize your impact.

Getting there: From the Intersection Rock Junction, drive 0.1 mile south and turn left at the Barker Dam/ Keys Ranch Road. Drive 0.6 mile to the Echo "T" junction, then bear right on the Barker Dam Road. From the Echo T, drive 0.8 mile and turn right onto the dirt Queen Valley Road. This turn is just before you get to the large Barker Dam parking area on the left. Go 0.1 mile down this dirt road and turn left, then go 0.3 mile to where the road ends at the Wall Street Mill parking area (GPS: N34° 01.685' / W116° 08.323'). There is an outhouse at the parking area.

Wonderland of Rocks

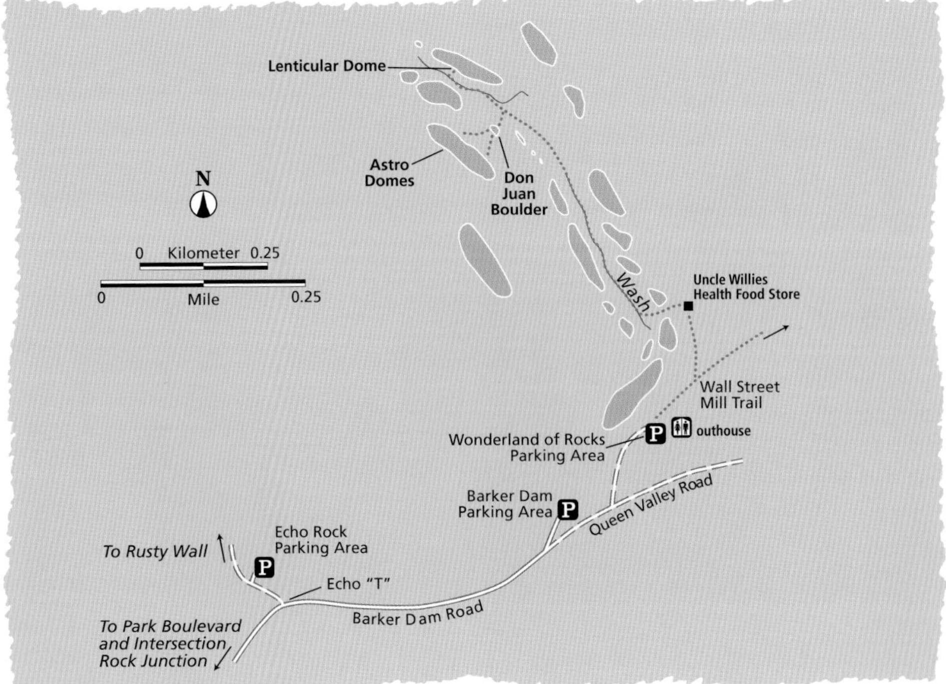

ASTRO DOMES

The Astro Domes are two massive rock formations with some of the tallest faces in Joshua Tree National Park. The rock is very high quality and offers some of the best face climbing in the park.

Finding the crags: From the parking area, walk northeast on the Wall Street Mill Trail for about 100 yards, then turn left and walk another 100 yards to the ruins of an old building (known as "Uncle Willies Health Food Store"). Make a sharp turn left (west) through a gap in the trees, and you'll come out into a broad sandy wash in a canyon that runs north–south. Turn right (north) and follow a trail in the wash for about 400 yards until the canyon opens up into a broad valley. Soon you'll see the massive hulk of the Astro Domes to your left. When you come to a fork in the trail (GPS: N34° 02.238' / W116° 08.560'), take the left fork and walk for another 300 yards, looking for a 50-foot-high boulder to your left over a low rock ridge. This is the Don Juan Boulder. Make a sharp left turn (GPS: N34° 02.331' / W116° 08.692') and walk about 200 feet to reach the Don Juan Boulder (GPS N34° 02.295' / W116° 08.731'). From here you'll have a good view of the Astro Domes. For the South Astro Dome, head up and left. For the North Astro Dome, up and right.

Astro Domes Overview

South Astro Dome—East Face

This tall cliff gets sun in the morning and shade in the late afternoon. GPS coordinates are included with individual route descriptions.

1. Hex Marks the Poot (5.8+) **Pitch 1:** Climb the classic widening crack (5.7+) that will test your technique from hands, to fists, to off-width—all in one pitch! Gear anchor. **Pro:** to 5 inches (#5 camalot or equivalent). Rappel from slings, or continue. **Pitch 2:** Jam the arching finger crack (5.8). **Pro:** Small to medium cams. Rap from slings, or continue. **Pitch 3:** For a third pitch that takes you to the top, do the last pitch of a route called Primal Flake. Climb up the flakes, undercling left out a roof (5.8+), then climb up and right to the top. Gear anchor.

Dave Evans wrote about *Hex Marks the Poot:* "I free-soloed this route in 1974 and found a #11 Hexentric at the start of the off-width. I assumed that I had done the first ascent since there weren't any anchors on top and the downclimb turned out to be as hard as the climb! I figured that the Hex marked the bail point (the 'poot') of whoever tried the route first."

South Astro Dome—East Face

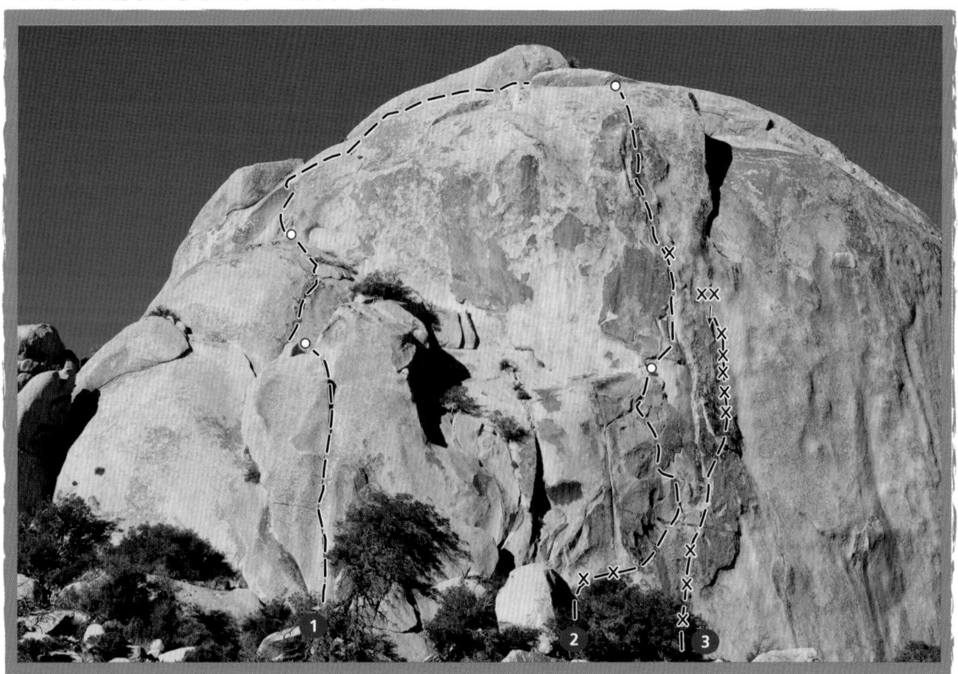

Route GPS: N34° 02.262' / W116° 08.797'. **Descent:** Make two 100-foot rappels from the top of *My Laundry* or *Breakfast of Champions.*

2. Strike It Rich (5.10a PG/R) While the first pitch isn't all that great, the second pitch has some bold and truly spectacular face climbing. **Pitch 1:** (5.10a) Face climb past two bolts, then traverse right and up to easy (5.5) but unprotected climbing. Belay on a ledge up and left (less than perfect gear anchor, .75 to 2 inches), or climb up and right to the bolt anchor on *Naked Singularity.* This pitch has swing potential for the follower after the second bolt. **Pitch 2:** Climb the exciting vertical face (5.10a) using some thin to medium nuts, one bolt, and a couple of tied-off horns for pro. Gear anchor (thin cams). Route GPS: N34° 02.289' / W116° 08.781'. **Descent:** Make two single-rope rappels from the top of *My Laundry* or *Breakfast of Champions.* **Pro:** single rack from # 3 stopper to 3.5-inch cam.

3. Naked Singularity (5.11c) **Pitch 1:** This route follows a series of features and edges on beautiful rock. Begin about 30 feet right of *Strike It Rich* and climb straight up past three bolts, moving right to a fourth bolt, then up past four more bolts to a bolted belay. Rappel 100 feet from here, or continue up *Strike It Rich* to the top for an ultra classic excursion. Route GPS: N34° 02.289' / W116° 08.781'. **Pro:** a few 1- to 2-inch cams between the bolts.

South Astro Dome—Northeast Face

This spectacular face gets morning sun and afternoon shade. Crag GPS: N34° 02.319' / W116° 08.808'

1. My Laundry (5.10a) **Pitch 1:** Begin from blocks about 50 feet left of *Solid Gold.* Climb the steep slab on thin edges (5.10a) past three bolts, then hand traverse right on a crack (1.5- and 3-inch cam) to a 2-bolt anchor (optional belay/rappel). Continue up and right (5.7 R) to reach a bolt, then climb to a bolt belay. **Pitch 2:** Climb a beautiful dihedral to the top. Bolt anchor. **Descent:** Two less than 100-foot rappels, or one less than 200-foot rappel.

2. Solid Gold (5.10b PG) A Joshua Tree classic. Bring your edging shoes for this one. **Pitch 1:** Steep, sustained 5.10 edging on orange rock leads past seven bolts. The top section is a wee bit runout. 2-bolt anchor. **Pitch 2:** Climb the flake on the left, moving left (5.10a) to reach a bolt. Climb up to a knob you can sling for pro, then climb past a bolt (5.9) up to a horizontal thin crack. Traverse left (5.10a) for about 30 feet, then climb past a bolt up to the summit. Gear anchor (1.25 to 1.75 inches). **Pro:** thin nuts to 1.75 inches. **Descent:** Rappel *My Laundry* or *Breakfast of Champions.*

South Astro Dome—Northeast Face, Left Side

3. Middle Age Crisis (5.11a PG) Very high quality. Begin about 20 feet right of *Solid Gold* and climb up to a bolt (shared with *Middle Age Crazy*), then move up and left (5.9 PG) to a second bolt. Continue past five more bolts up to a 2-bolt belay/rappel anchor (less than 100 feet).

4. Middle Age Crazy (5.11d PG) Same start as *Middle Age Crisis*, but at the first bolt move right up to a second bolt, then follow a flake that leads up and right. Climb straight up (sustained 5.11) past four more bolts, then continue past three more bolts on slightly runout face climbing to the top. **Pro:** to 2.5 inches. **Descent:** Rappel *My Laundry* or *Breakfast of Champions*.

South Astro Dome—Northeast Face, Right Side

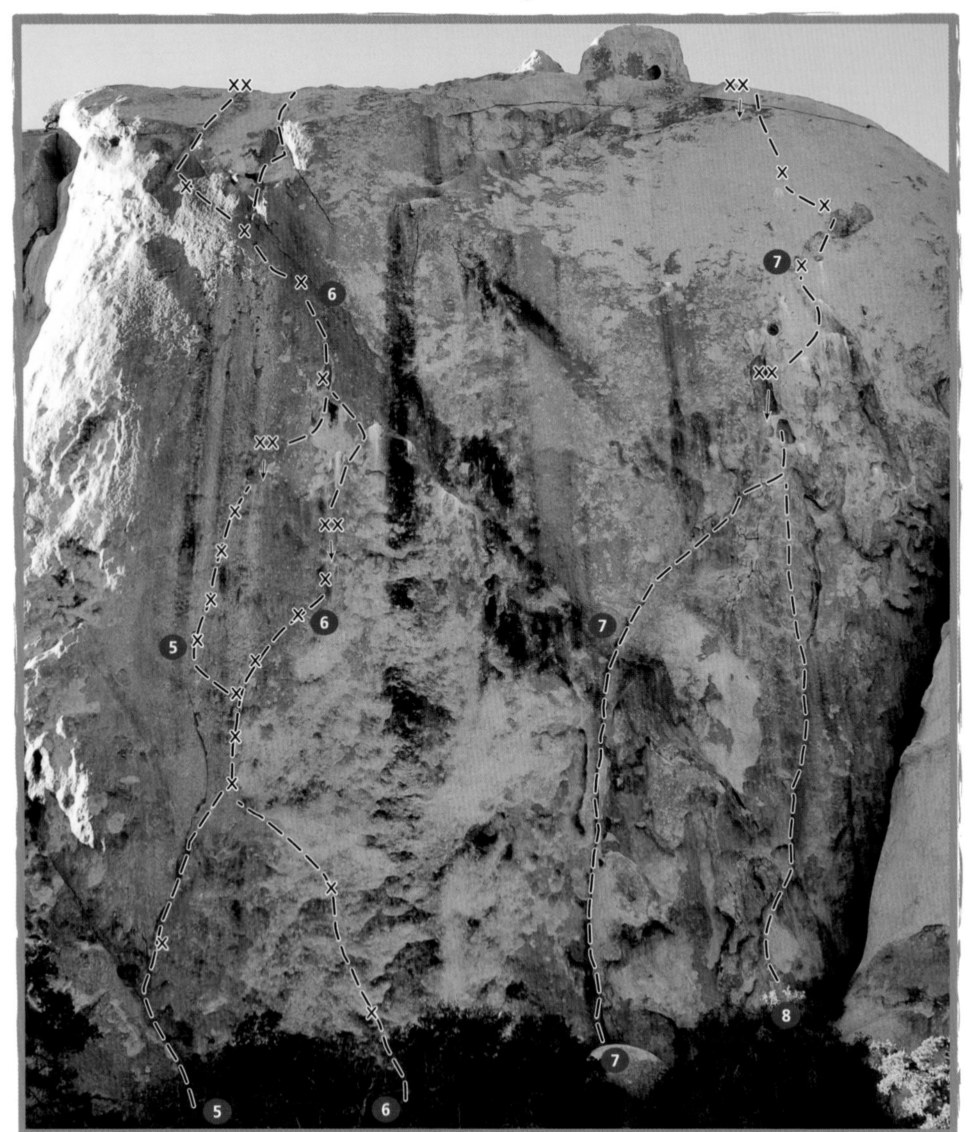

5. Middle Age Savage (5.12b) Excellent rock quality. The crux is the final move to the belay. Begin 30 feet left of *Such a Savage* on a ramp. Move straight up past a bolt (5.9) and up a crack, joining *Such a Savage* for three bolts, then cut left and climb a steep face past four more bolts to a 2-bolt belay/rappel anchor (85 feet). Rap from here, or continue up *Such a Savage*'s second pitch (5.10a). **Pro:** optional medium piece for the crack after the first bolt, a few medium pieces for the second pitch.

6. Such a Savage (5.11a) A Joshua Tree classic, especially when combined with the less-scary *Middle Age Savage* start. **Pitch 1:** Climb a slab (5.10a R) past two widely spaced bolts, then move up and left and climb a steeper face on excellent rock past six closely spaced bolts to a slim stance at a 2-bolt belay/rappel anchor (80 feet). **Pitch 2:** Climb up and left (5.10a) past four bolts to the top. At the third bolt you can also climb straight up to the top. Rappel *My Laundry* or *Breakfast of Champions*. **Pro:** a few medium pieces to 2.5 inches for the second pitch.

7. Breakfast of Champions (5.9- PG/R) **Pitch 1:** Start with a short off-width (or easy ramp on the right), jam a hand crack (5.9-), climb the flake, then face climb up and right to a 2-bolt stance. **Pitch 2:** Climb the airy face up to a bolt, then run it out (5.8 R) up to a second bolt. Move left (5.9-) then up a slab past a third bolt to the top. 2-bolt anchor (80 feet). **Descent:** Rappel the route with two less than 100-foot rappels.

8. Piggle Pugg (5.10c) Face climb and lieback the thin crack in a small right-facing dihedral. A demanding lead, but easy to toprope from the *Breakfast of Champions* anchor. Bolt anchor (80 feet). **Pro:** to 2 inches.

North Astro Dome—Northeast Face

One of the most impressive faces in all of Joshua Tree, with some of the best rock.

Finding the crag: From the Don Juan Boulder, hike up and right on slabs to reach the base. Crag GPS: N34° 02.327' / W116° 08.832'

Descent: From the summit bolt anchor, downclimb left (south) about 30 feet to a bolt anchor. Rappel 165 feet with two ropes, or make two 80-foot rappels (to another bolt anchor) to reach the base.

1. Figures on a Landscape (5.10b PG) A true classic with superb rock and outstanding climbing. **Pitch 1:** Begin from the left and walk right on a ledge/ramp to reach the first bolt. Climb up and right (5.10b), then weave straight up (5.10-) past four more bolts. At the fifth bolt, make a long traverse straight right (5.9) to a 3-bolt anchor (optional hanging belay), then continue right (5.10b/c) up to another 2-bolt anchor at a nice stance. **Pitch 2:** Climb an airy face (5.9 PG) past one bolt up to a right-leaning crack (2.5-inch cam) that leads to a nice ledge. Gear anchor (nuts and small to medium cams). **Pitch 3:** (5.9) Stem and jam the short dihedral to the top (2- to 3-inch pro). Bolt anchor. **Pro:** single set of cams from 1 to 3 inches, medium stoppers.

2. Astroturf (5.11a R) **Pitch 1:** Climb *Figures on a Landscape* to its fifth bolt, then climb straight up to a flake (5.10a R), which is liebacked to a 2-bolt belay/rappel stance (113 feet). You can make two less than 100-foot rappels from here. **Pitch 2:** (6 bolts) Make a tough move on the right (5.11a) to start, then climb up and left on a patina rail, finishing with some delicate face moves (5.10-) and a slab finish. Bolt anchor. **Pro:** a few cams from 1.25 to 3 inches for the first pitch.

North Astro Dome—Northeast Face

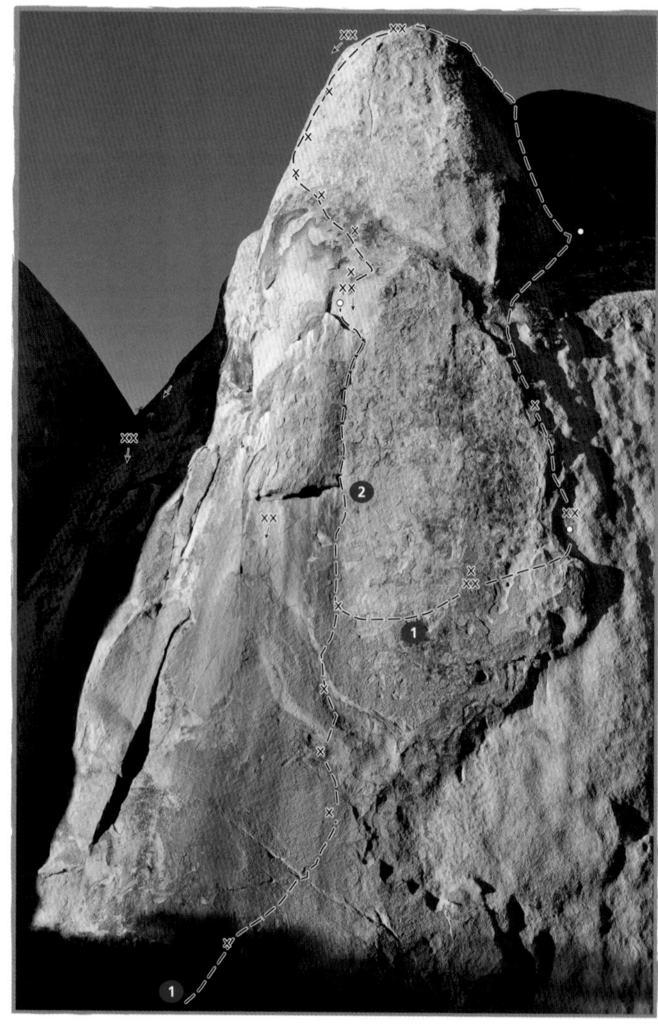

North Astro Dome—North Face

Finding the crag: From the base of *Figures on a Landscape,* walk right along the base of the cliff for a few hundred feet.

Descent: Rappel as for *Figures on a Landscape,* with two rappels of less than 100 feet each.

1. Gunslinger (5.12) One of the longest routes in the park. The first pitch is a bit flaky, but after that the quality of the rock is excellent. Begin about 200 feet right of *Figures on a Landscape,* just right of the lowest point on the North Astro Dome. **Pitch 1:** The "Moguls" pitch, 5.12a/b. (8 bolts). 5.9 up to the first bolt, 5.7 R to the second bolt, then up the moguls (5.10) to steeper, well-protected slab climbing (5.11b above the fourth bolt and 5.12 above the sixth bolt). Traverse left (5.10a) to a bolt belay. **Pitch 2:** Steeper edging on perfect rock (5.11b) up and left past four bolts to another bolt belay. **Pitch 3:** The "Headwall" pitch. Crank a height-dependent and bouldery move right off the belay (5.12a/b/c, V4/5), then follow edges up the gently overhanging wall (5.11+) past seven bolts. Belay on a narrow ledge with a bolt anchor. **Pitch 4:** The "Coral Corner." Tough stemming (5.12-) past two bolts in the corrugated corner leads to easier climbing past another bolt to the top. There was a fixed pin between the second and third bolts on the first ascent. Gear anchor. **Pro:** to 3 inches.

North Astro Dome—North Face

2. Unknown Soldier (5.11b) **Pitch 1:** (5.10c) Climb the featured face on excellent rock past three bolts (moving right from the second bolt, 5.10c) to a 2-bolt anchor. **Pitch 2:** A tough move (5.11b) at the first bolt leads to easier friction slab climbing past five more bolts to the top. 2-bolt belay/rappel anchor. **Descent:** Rappel the route with two ropes (more than 100 feet), or top out and rappel off the east side (two single-rope rappels). **Pro:** a few medium pieces plus slings for tie-offs on pitch 1.

North Astro Dome—North Face

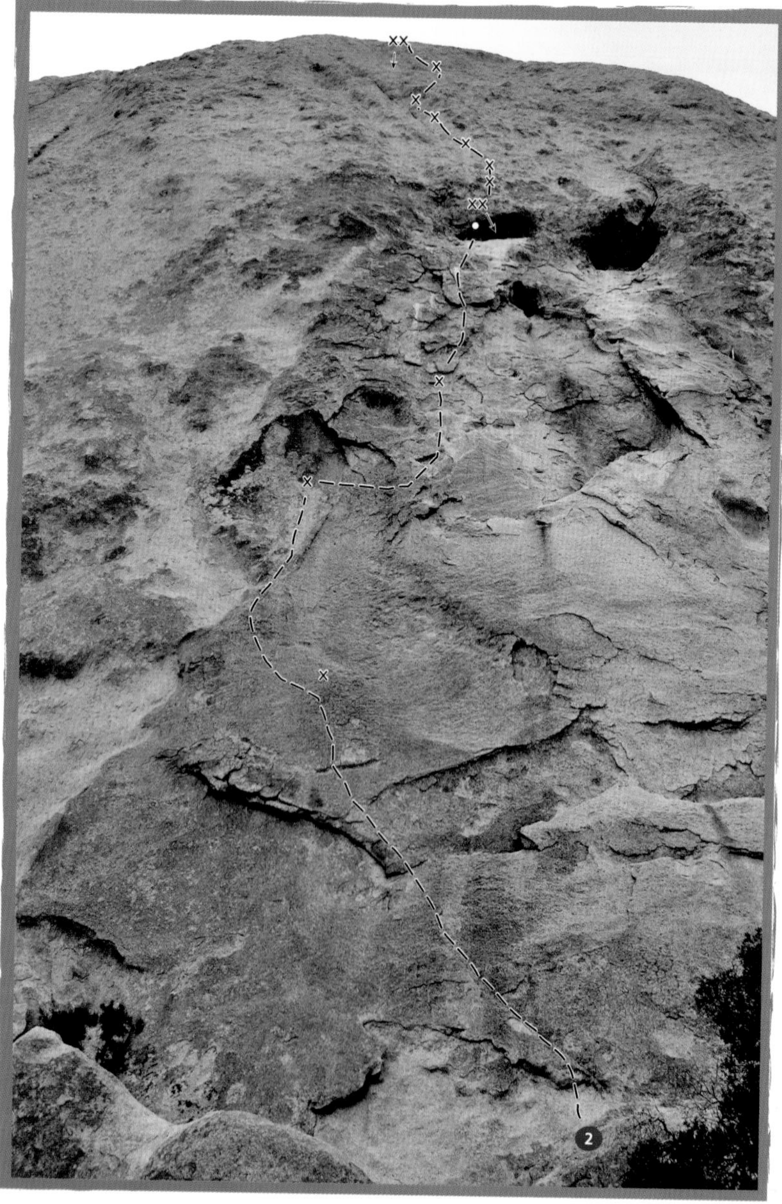

LENTICULAR DOME

This large dome faces south and gets a lot of sun, making it a good choice for cool days. The climbs are popular and well worth the long approach.

Finding the crag: From the parking area, walk northeast on the Wall Street Mill Trail for about 100 yards, then turn left and walk another 100 yards to the ruins of an old building (known as "Uncle Willies Health Food Store"). Make a sharp turn left (west) through a gap in the trees, and you'll come out into a broad sandy wash in a canyon that runs north–south. Turn right (north) and follow a trail in the wash for about 400 yards until the canyon opens up into a broad valley. Soon you'll see the massive hulk of the Astro Domes to your left. When you come to a fork in the trail (GPS: N34° 02.238' / W 116 08.560'), take the left fork. You'll soon see Lenticular Dome straight ahead to the northwest. The trail drops slightly into a small drainage that soon becomes a sandy wash. Shortly the wash is filled with small boulders that require a bit of boulder-hopping. For the easiest approach, follow the wash to a point just past the Lenticular Dome formation (GPS: N34° 02.517' / W116° 08.950'), then turn right and go up to the base of the cliff (some 3rd class). Approach time is forty-five minutes to one hour. Crag GPS: N34° 02.533' / W116° 08.933'

Lenticular Dome Approach

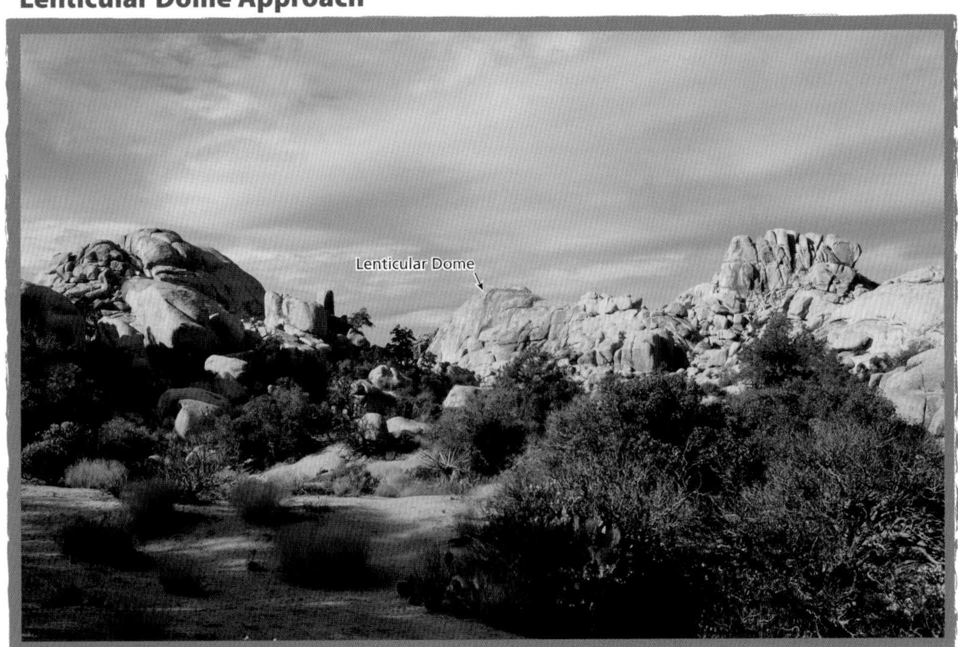

Lenticular Dome

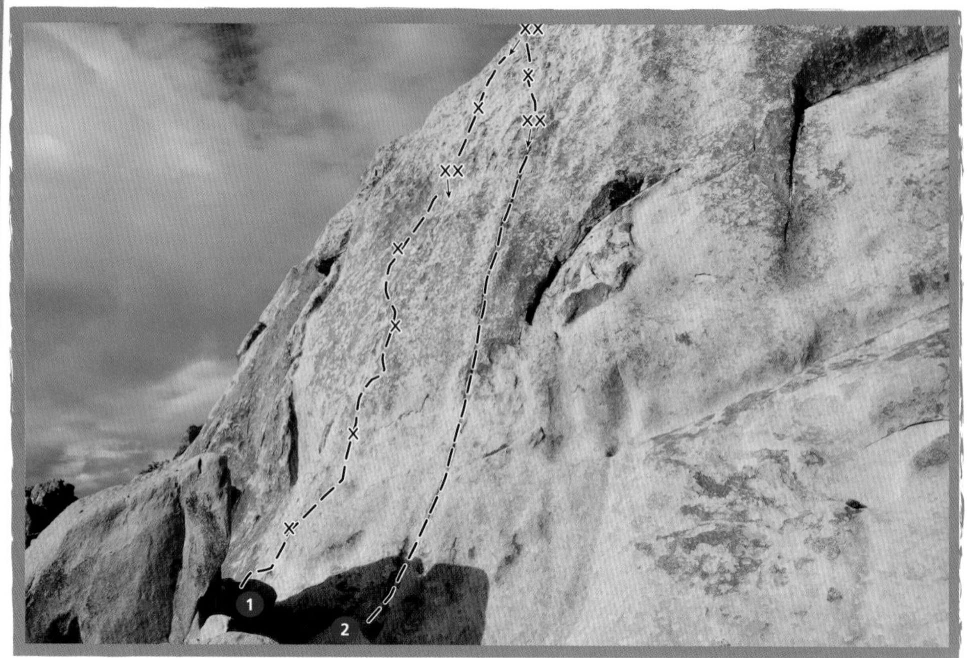

1. Dazed and Confused (5.9 PG) Excellent route. **Pitch 1:** Friction up the face past four bolts (5.9) to a bolt anchor (90 feet). **Pitch 2:** Climb a little left-facing corner, then up the face past a bolt to the top and another bolt anchor. **Descent:** Two single-rope rappels (less than 100 feet) down the route.

2. Mental Physics (5.7) One of the best 5.7 routes in the park. **Pitch 1:** Jam the well-protected crack up to a 2-bolt belay/rappel anchor. Rappel from here with two ropes or one 70-meter rope (110 feet), or continue to the top. **Pitch 2:** Climb the slab past one bolt to the top. Gear anchor. **Descent:** Rappel down *Dazed and Confused,* or scramble off to the right (3rd or 4th class), down slabs to a gully that leads back around to the base. **Pro:** to 3 inches.

9.

Cap Rock

Cap Rock is a huge formation with excellent-quality rock. Just before the parking lot you can see the "cap rock," balanced precariously on the summit. *Catch a Falling Star* faces south and is a good choice on cold days. The *Ayatolla* is in the shade in the afternoon.

Getting there: From the Intersection Rock Junction, drive 1.6 miles south and turn right at Keys View Road. From the North Entrance, drive 14.7 miles and turn left. Go 0.2 mile and turn left into a large parking lot with an outhouse (GPS: N33° 59.359' / W116° 09.821').

Cap Rock

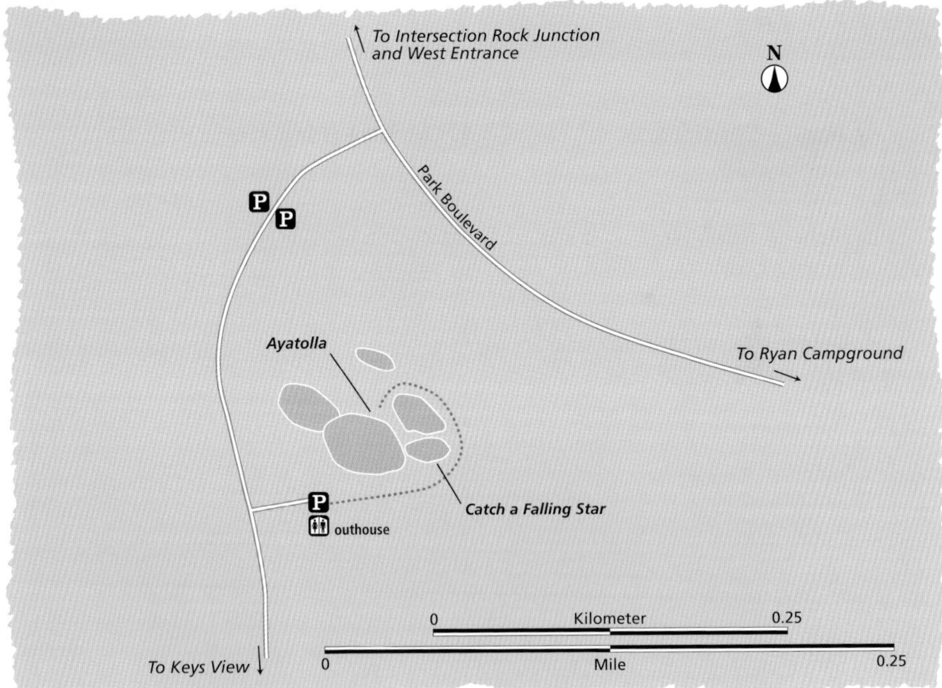

Cap Rock—South Face

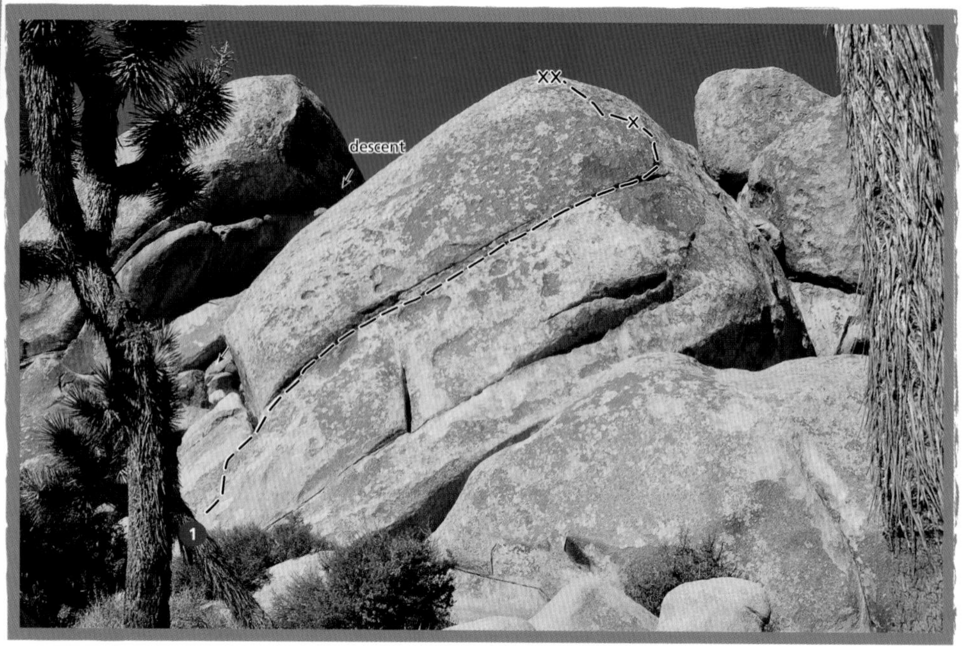

Cap Rock—South Face

Finding the crag: From the parking area, walk around the right (south) side of the formation for about 300 feet. *Catch a Falling Star* will be on your left.

Descent: Scramble (3rd class) down a gully on the left side.

1. Catch a Falling Star (5.8) A classic hand traverse. When the crack ends, face climb past a bolt to the top. 2-bolt anchor. **Pro:** double rack to 2 inches.

Cap Rock—Upper Northeast Face

Cap Rock—Upper Northeast Face

This cliff faces northeast and gets morning sun and afternoon shade.

Finding the crag: From the Cap Rock parking lot, walk around the right (south) of the formation until you can see the upper northeast face, then scramble (3rd class) up to the base.

1. The Ayatolla (5.11c) This route begins from the middle of an aesthetic amphitheater on the upper northeast face. Climb a thin crack up to a fingertip lieback seam with three bolts. 2-bolt anchor on top. **Descent:** Walk 30 feet left to a 2-bolt rap station. **Pro:** to 1.5 inches.

Ryan Campground and Headstone Rock

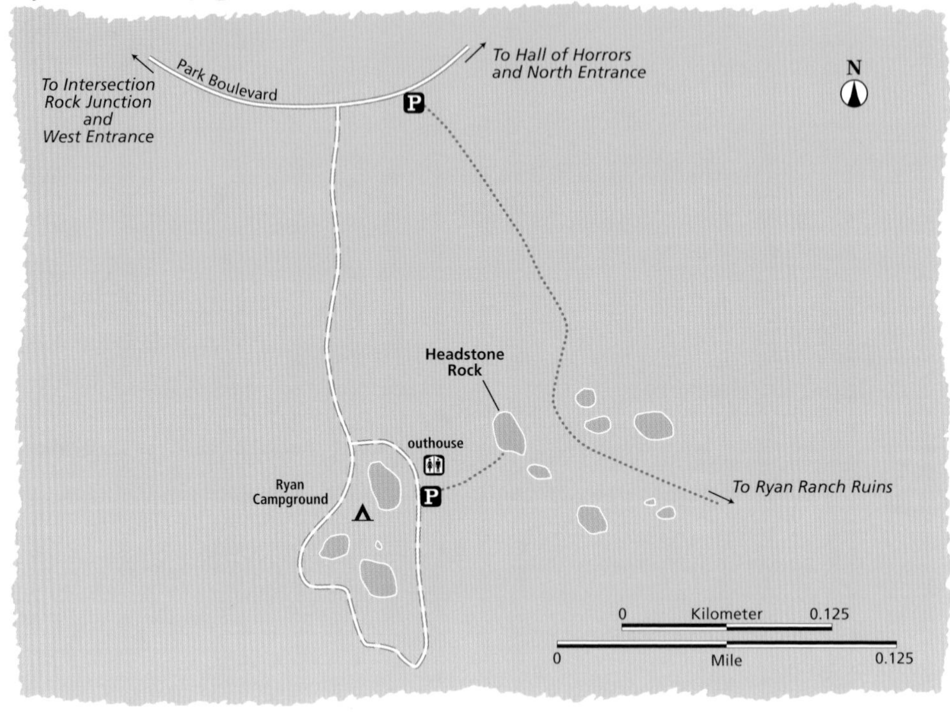

10. Ryan Campground

Headstone Rock near Ryan Campground is the iconic spire of Joshua Tree, with a fantastic summit. It is a huge block perched high on a rock pedestal 200 yards east of Ryan Campground. The crag is very popular—it's wise to scope it out from the parking area to see if anyone's waiting to climb. The south side is in the sun most of the day.

Getting there: From the Intersection Rock Junction, drive 2.2 miles south and turn right into Ryan Campground. From the North Entrance, drive 14.1 miles and turn left. Follow the one-way loop all the way around to the left (east) side to a small parking area (GPS N33° 59.028' / W116° 09.231'). A marked climber's trail leads to the formation. Scramble (3rd class) up the boulders on the west side to the base. Crag GPS: N33° 59.052' / W116° 09.148'

Descent: Rappel 50 feet from bolts down either the north or south sides. If you rap off the north side, there is a bit of downclimbing required to get back to the base.

Headstone Rock Overview

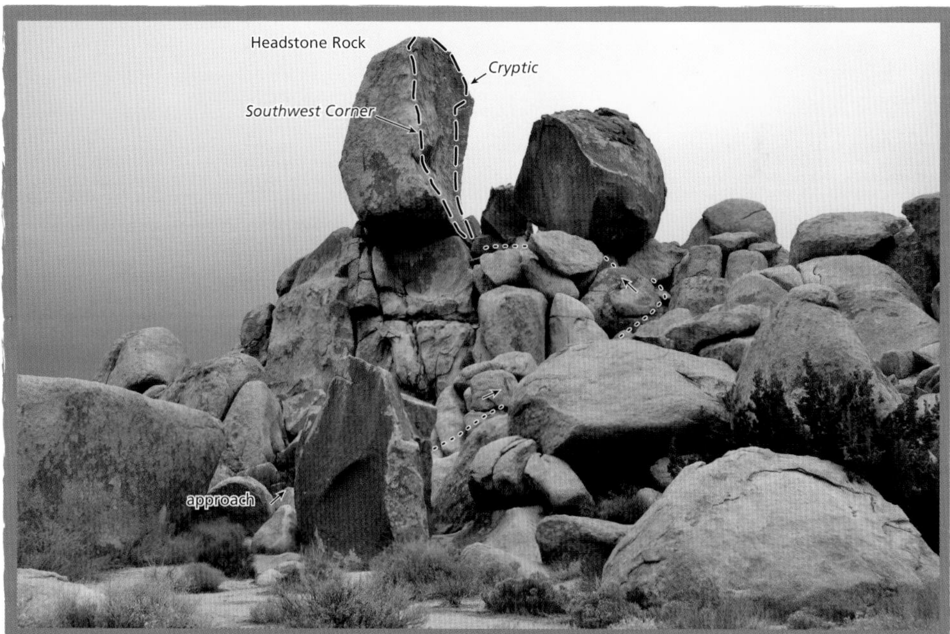

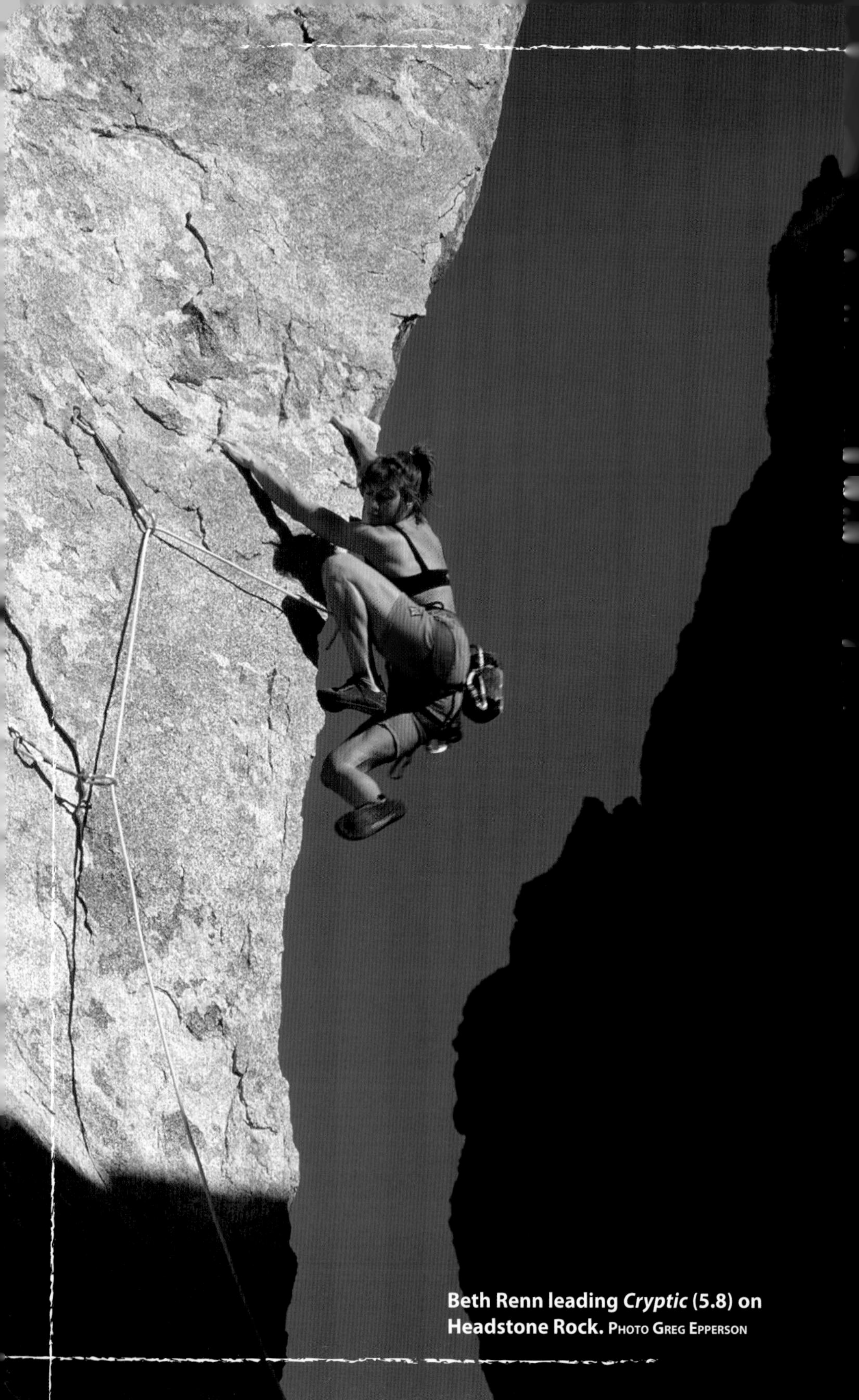

Beth Renn leading *Cryptic* (5.8) on Headstone Rock. PHOTO GREG EPPERSON

Headstone Rock—South Side

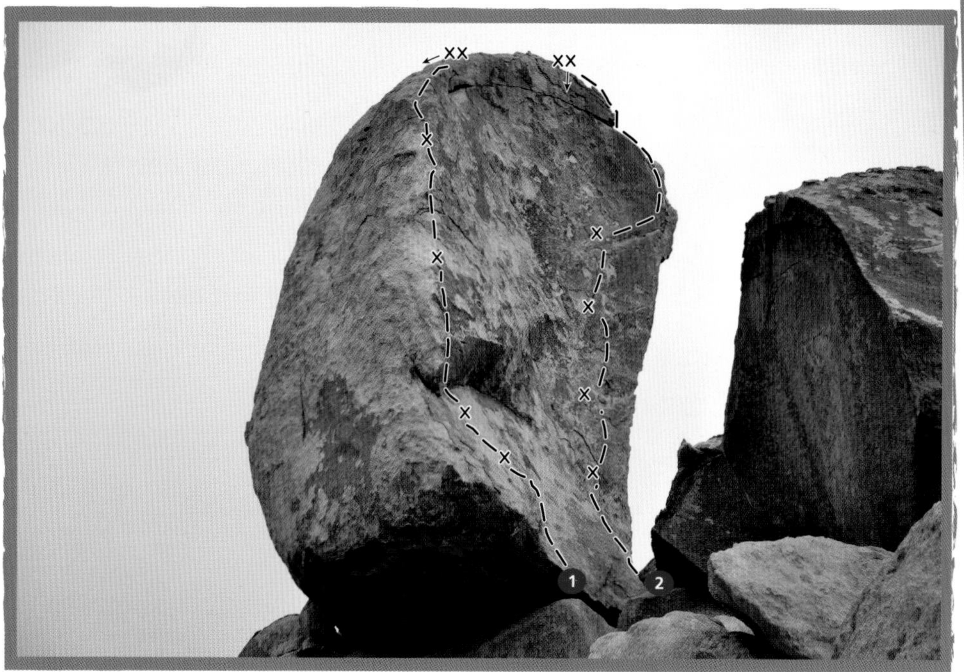

HEADSTONE ROCK

Headstone Rock—South Side

1. Southwest Corner (5.6) A short route with surprising exposure. Climb past four bolts up the left (southwest) arête. Bolt anchor on top.

2. Cryptic (5.8) Sport. Tricky face climbing past four bolts up the right (southeast) arête. Bolt anchor on top.

Like the Lost Arrow Spire in Yosemite Valley, which was first "ascended" by climbers tossing a rope over the tip, then prussiking up to the top, the first climbers to stand on top of Headstone Rock did so by employing an elaborate feat of rope shenanigans rather than by climbing prowess. In 1956 Bob Boyle and Rod Smith reached the summit by prussiking up a rope they managed to toss over the top of the rock. The first actual free climb of Headstone Rock would come two years later, in 1958, when Mark Powell and Bill "Dolt" Feurer climbed the classic *Southwest Corner* route. Both climbers were also involved in early attempts to make the first ascent of Yosemite's El Capitan. Headstone Rock derives its name from the nearby graves of several nineteenth century gold miners, one of whom who was murdered in 1893 over a disputed claim at Joshua Tree's Desert Queen mine.

Headstone Rock—North Side

Headstone Rock—North Side

1. The Cutting Edge (5.13b) Sport. Four bolts on the dramatic northeast arête. Bolt anchor.

In the early 1990s Scott Cosgrove put up some of the hardest routes in America, including Joshua Tree's first 5.14a, *Integrity,* located on the south face of Turtle Rock. *The Cutting Edge* is one of his signature routes from that era.

11.

Hall of Horrors

Easy access with a variety of both north- and south-facing cliffs characterizes the Hall of Horrors.

Getting there: From the Intersection Rock Junction, drive south (the road eventually curves east) for 3.1 miles and turn left into the large Hall of Horrors parking area. From the North Entrance, drive 13.2 miles and turn right. There is an outhouse at the parking area (GPS: N33° 59.917' / W116° 08.699'). Marked climber's trails lead to the various crags.

Hall of Horrors and Saddle Rock

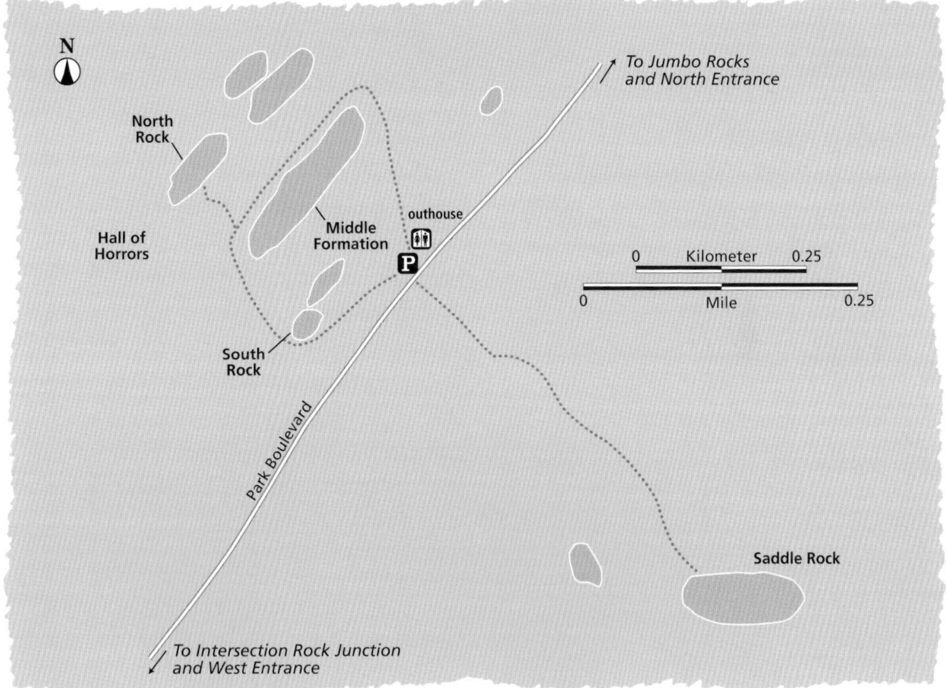

South Rock—Southeast Face

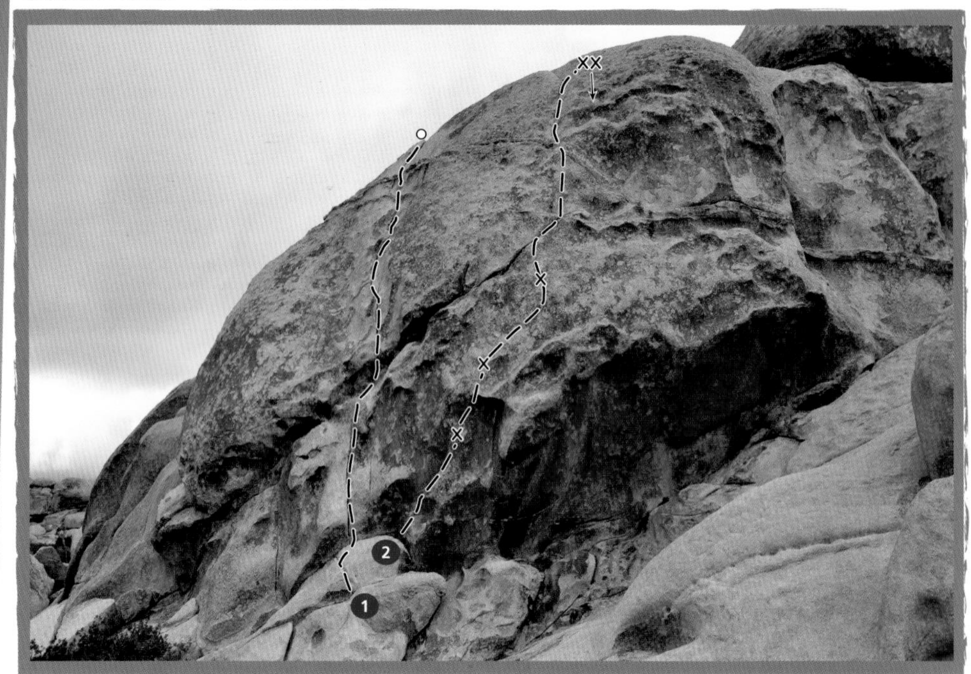

SOUTH ROCK

South Rock—Southeast Face

Finding the crag: From the parking area, walk west on a marked climber's trail that leads directly to this southeast-facing cliff. It is in the sun until late in the day, making it a good choice for cool-weather days. Crag GPS: N33° 59.853' / W116° 08.757'

1. Lazy Days (5.7) Steep jamming and liebacking with good pro. Gear anchor. **Descent:** Downclimb (3rd class) directly behind the route, then head left down a slab to the base. **Pro:** to 3 inches.

2. Cactus Flower (5.11b) Climb the steep face past three bolts, then up a crack to a 2-bolt belay/rappel anchor. There is also a bolt for a 5.12 direct start. **Pro:** to 2 inches.

South Rock—Northeast Face

South Rock—Northeast Face

Finding the crag: From the parking area, walk west on a marked climber's trail that leads directly to the cliff. It is in the sun in the morning and the shade in the afternoon. Crag GPS: N33° 59.873' / W116° 08.794'

1. Dog Day Afternoon (5.10b PG) Climb a steep arête past four bolts on nice edges, then stem up a dihedral past one more bolt to a ledge with a 2-bolt belay/rappel anchor. **Pro:** 2- to 3-inch cam for the start of the dihedral.

Middle Formation—North Face

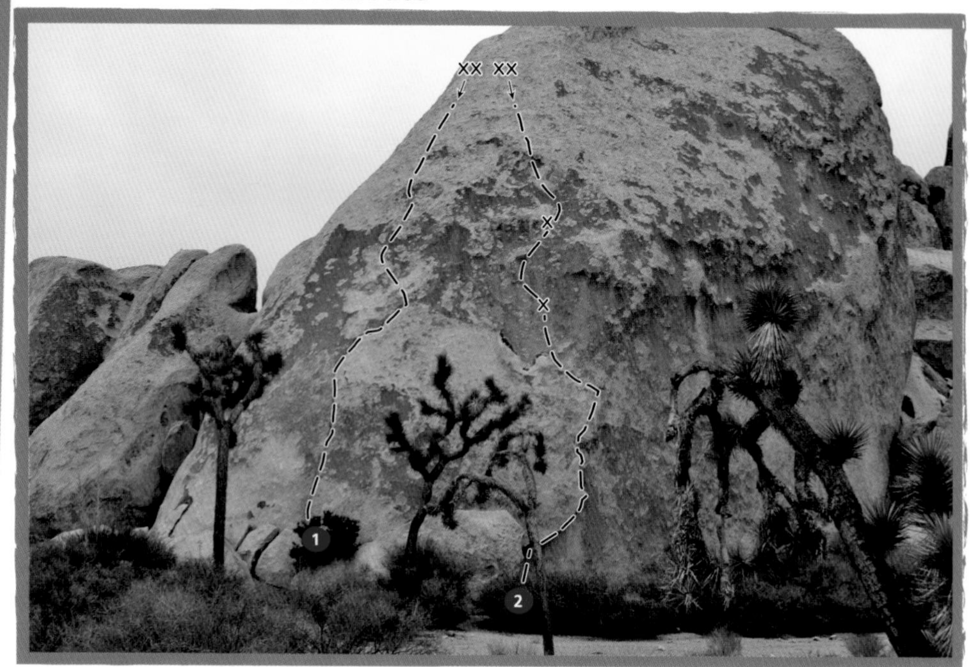

MIDDLE FORMATION

Middle Formation—North Face

Finding the crag: From the parking area, follow the marked climber's trail that leads northeast, around the right side of the middle formation. You'll come to the northeast corner first; the *Exorcist* is about 150 yards to the right. These climbs get very little sun in the winter. Crag GPS: N33° 59.873' / W116° 08.794'

1. Lickety Splits (5.7 X) Climb a splitter finger crack to an unprotected face (5.6 X) up to a 2-bolt belay/rappel anchor (80 feet). **Pro:** to 1.5 inches.

2. Diamond Dogs (5.10a) Classic climbing on excellent rock. Start with an undercling/lieback on a flake, then move left onto the face and wind past two bolts to the top. 2-bolt belay/rappel anchor (80 feet). The start is height dependent. **Pro:** a medium cam or two for the move off the flake.

Middle Formation—Northwest Face

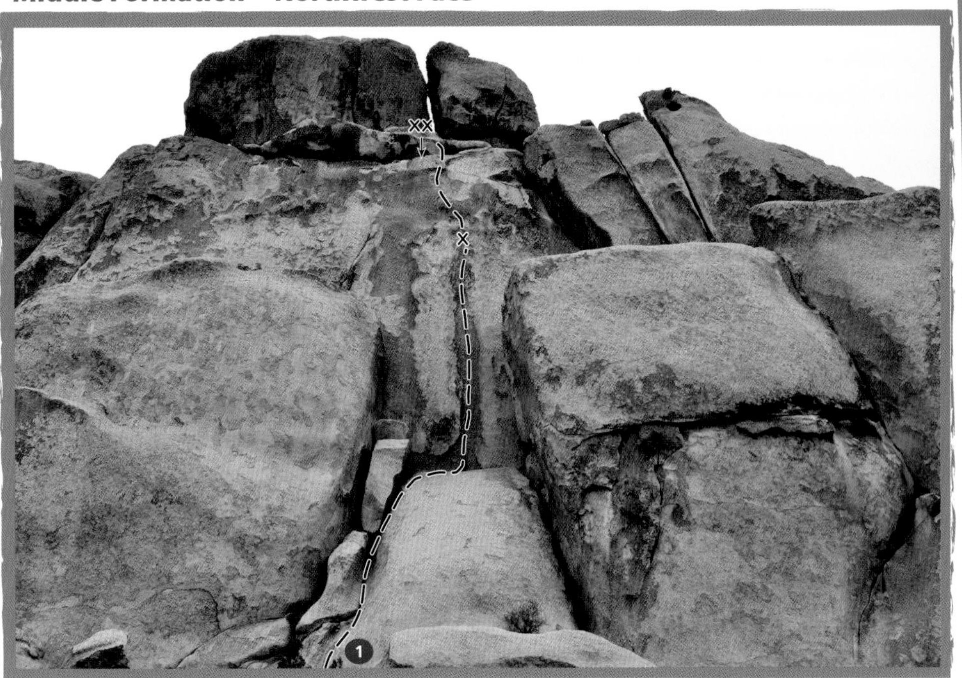

Middle Formation—Northwest Face

1. Exorcist (5.10a) A beautiful, striking line. Begin from a ledge in a recess about 40 feet up. Finger jam and lieback the thin crack, then face climb past one bolt up to a ledge with a 2-bolt belay/rappel anchor (100 feet). Route GPS: N34° 00.001′ / W116° 08.807′. **Pro:** to 2 inches.

North Rock—East Face

NORTH ROCK

North Rock—East Face

Finding the crag: From the parking area, follow the marked climber's trail that leads northeast, around the right side of the middle formation. Walk past *Diamond Dogs* and *Exorcist,* and *Jane's Addiction* will be on the wall to your right. This climb faces east and is in the sun in the morning and the shade in the afternoon. Crag GPS: N34° 00.026' W116° 08.832'

Descent/access to the top: Scramble (3rd class) on the left side.

1. Jane's Addiction (5.11b) Sport. A powerful reach past the first bolt (5.11-) leads to steep face climbing on nice patina past three more bolts (5.11b) to a 2-bolt anchor.

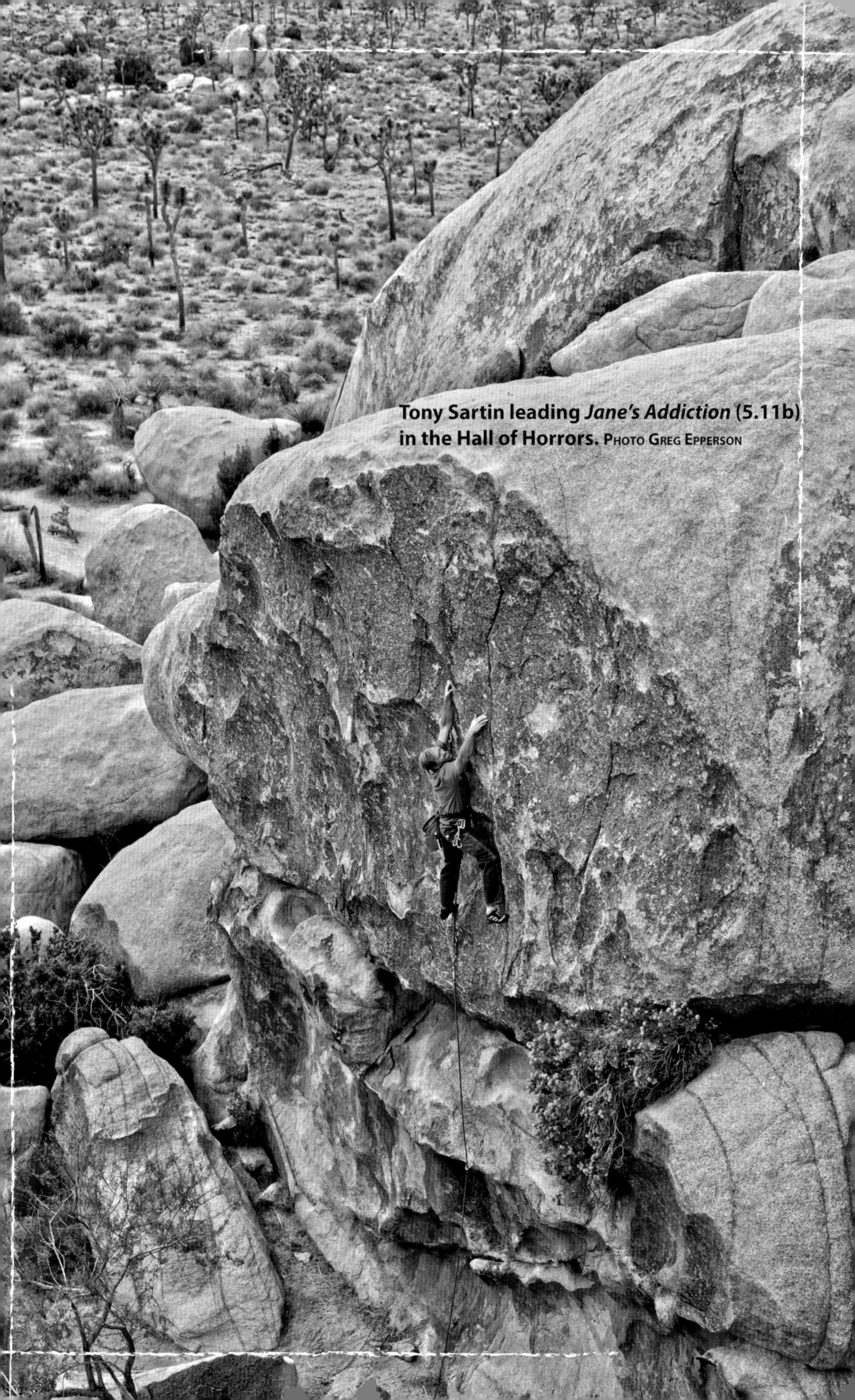

Tony Sartin leading *Jane's Addiction* (5.11b) in the Hall of Horrors. PHOTO GREG EPPERSON

Brett Pinar leading the first pitch of the incredible moderate face climb *Walk on the Wild Side* (5.8), Saddle Rocks. PHOTO GREG EPPERSON

12.

Saddle Rock

The largest rock formation in all of Joshua Tree, Saddle Rock is known for its classic face climbs. The moderate multi-pitch *Right On* is Joshua Tree's longest route. The main face is in the shade in the morning and the sun in the afternoon.

Getting there: (See overview map on page 117). From the Intersection Rock Junction, drive 3.1 miles south and turn left into the large Hall of Horrors parking area. From the North Entrance, drive 13.2 miles and turn right. There is an outhouse at the parking area. A marked climber's trail leads southeast directly to the rock. Hiking time is about ten minutes. Crag GPS: N33° 59.702' / W116° 08.464'

Descent: Descent information is given with each route.

Saddle Rock Overview

Saddle Rock—Northeast Face

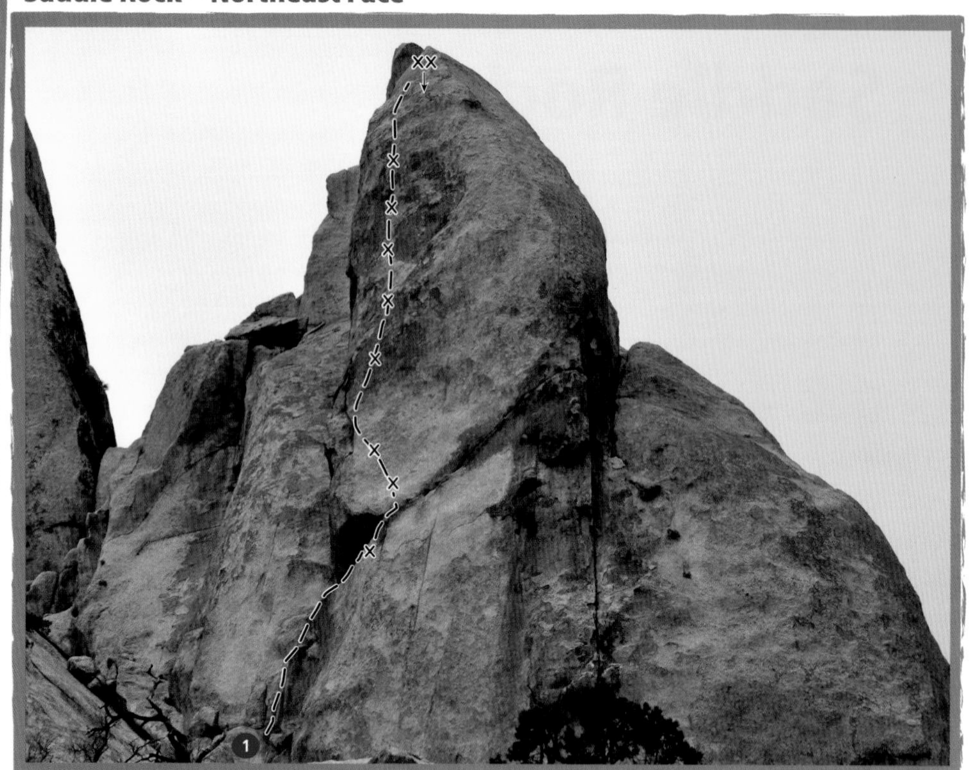

Saddle Rock—Northeast Face

1. Space Mountain (5.10b) This exciting route climbs the face of a turret high on the left side of the formation. Begin in a left-facing corner, moving right on a ledge/ramp about 25 feet up. You'll pass a total of eight bolts on this wild and exposed pitch. The holds near the top are a bit loose, but this climb has a great location and fun moves. There is a 5.8 runout at the top. 2-bolt belay/rappel anchor. **Descent:** Rappel 120 feet with two ropes. **Pro:** small to medium stoppers plus a 1.75-inch cam.

Saddle Rock—North Face and Northwest Face

1. Where Have all the Cowboys Gone (5.10d) The second pitch has some superb face climbing and achieves a spectacular position. **Pitch 1:** Jam a finger crack (5.8) to a bolt that protects a face move (5.8) to easier but runout climbing up to a ledge with a 2-bolt belay/rappel anchor. **Pitch 2:** (9 bolts) Crank up a vertical wall (5.10d) to easier face climbing, then move left and up a friction slab (5.10b/c) to the top. 2-bolt belay/rappel anchor. **Descent:** Rappel the route with two single-rope rappels (90 feet and 70 feet), or rappel from the top to the ground with two ropes (165 feet). **Pro:** to 2 inches for the first pitch.

2. Santa Cruz (5.10a) Link these three routes for a multi-pitch classic. **Pitch 1:** (5.8) Climb the first pitch of *Where Have all the Cowboys Gone.* **Pitch 2:** (Santa Cruz) Move right over a small overhang, then up a slab past four bolts (5.9) to a 2-bolt belay/rappel anchor. To descend from here, rappel the route in two (less than 100 feet) rappels. **Pitch 3:** (called *R & R*) Jam the obvious finger/hand crack through a small overhang (5.10a). Gear anchor. **Descent:** You can downclimb to and rappel *Where Have all the Cowboys Gone,* or climb up to the finish of *Right On* and rap 100 feet down the back side. **Pro:** to 3 inches.

Saddle Rock—North Face

Saddle Rock—North Face

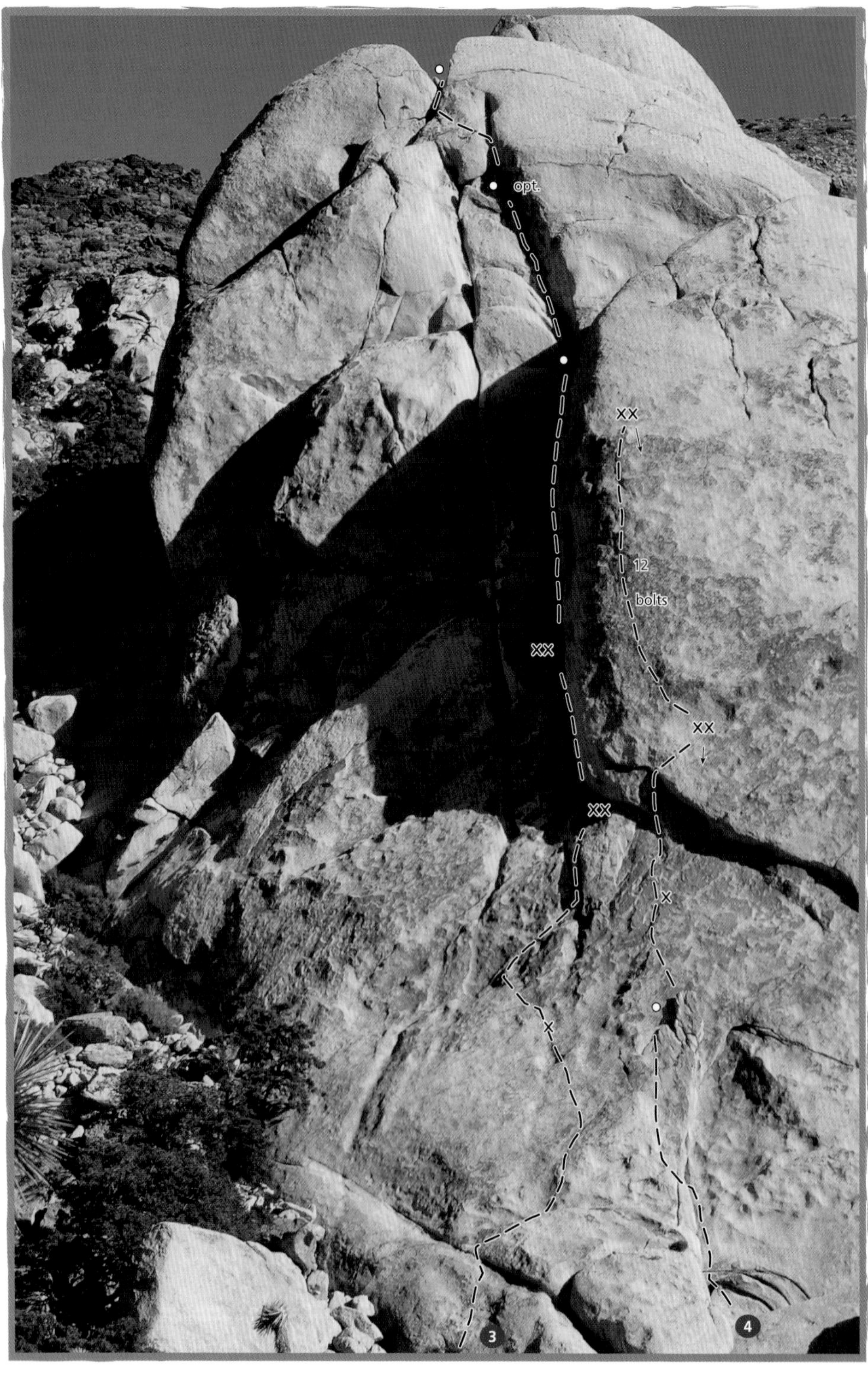

3. Right On (5.6 PG) Great variety and quality make this route a moderate classic. **Pitch 1:** (5.6) Climb an easy but unprotected slab up and right to a short, vertical crack, then climb the slab up to a bolt. From the bolt the easiest line is to move left about 10 feet, then up (5.6), then traverse right to a vertical crack that leads to a belay stance on a sloping ledge with a bolt anchor. It is significantly harder (5.8) if you climb straight up past the bolt, but better for your follower. **Pitch 2:** (5.5) Jam the short hand and fist crack up to a nice ledge with two bolts at the base of a chimney. **Pitch 3:** (5.6+) A tough entry move gets you into the chimney. Squirm your way up for about 50 feet; the angle then lessens considerably. Climb up to a belay area in a large, boulder-filled chasm on the right. Gear anchor. You can also climb the slab to the left of the chimney (5.5), but it is unprotected. **Pitch 4:** Climb a fun trough (5.3) for about a hundred feet, jam a hand crack over a bulge (5.4), move left across a face with a dike, then up to the "v notch" (you'll see a pointed boulder jutting out) and a belay at blocks. You can break this pitch into two shorter pitches for less rope drag if you belay at the top of the trough, below the hand crack. **Descent:** Downclimb (4th class) a short gully to a big ledge with a 2-bolt rappel anchor to the left (100-foot rappel). Scramble (3rd class) through boulders, staying well away from the cliff for the easiest descent back down to the base. **Pro:** to 3 inches, including several 2- to 3-inch pieces for pitch 2.

4. Silver Spur (5.12c) The third pitch is one of Joshua Tree's classic hard slabs. Start about 75 feet right of *Right On.* Climb a low-angle slab (4th class) just right of a right-facing corner up to a big ledge/ramp. **Pitch 1:** Go left, around the corner, then up a low-angle slab (5.5) to a belay at a small ledge with a block. **Pitch 2:** (5.10a) Climb up a steepening face to a bolt, then move left to a thin flake that leads to a left-facing corner. Follow this over a roof, then step right to a 2-bolt hanging belay. **Pitch 3:** (5.12) Up and left on very sustained slab climbing past twelve bolts to a 2-bolt anchor. **Descent:** Rappel the route with two ropes. **Pro:** to 3 inches.

Saddle Rock—Northwest Face

5. Harley Queen (5.10d) Start about 75 feet right of *Right On*. Climb a low-angle slab (4th class) just right of a right-facing corner up to a big ledge/ramp. **Pitch 1:** Walk right across this ledge to where it becomes more like a ramp, leading up and right and then blanking out. Continue right across a slab past two bolts (5.8) to the top of a left-facing corner. Belay on a small ledge with two bolts.

An alternative start is to climb a somewhat loose left-facing dihedral (5.7) directly from the base of the wall up to the bolt belay on top of the first pitch. **Pitch 2:** Climb up and left on a steepening slab to vertical face climbing past seven bolts to a 2-bolt belay/rappel anchor. **Descent:** Two single-rope rappels (less than 100 feet each) to the ground; with a 70-meter rope you can rap diagonally left to the big ledge/ramp.

Tony Sartin on the third pitch of *Silver Spur* (5.12c).

6. Walk on the Wild Side (5.8 PG) A real Joshua classic, but it's no sport climb, with some long runouts between the bolts. Start at a boulder that leans against the face (involves a little scrambling to get to). **Pitch 1:** Climb the slab past six bolts, using slings to reduce rope drag, with the crux moves up and right from the last bolt. (There is an optional 1-inch gear placement between bolts 4 and 5 that minimizes a swing for the follower.) Belay in a scoop with a 2-bolt anchor. **Pitch 2:** Climb straight up the slab (5.6) past four bolts, then traverse 20 feet left to a 2-bolt belay. **Pitch 3:** Easier climbing past two bolts to a good ledge with a 2-bolt belay/rappel anchor. Most parties rappel the route from here with two ropes. (There is an additional bolt rappel anchor to the right of *Walk on the Wild Side* that you can use if other parties are climbing the route.) Pitches 2 and 3 can be combined with a 60-meter rope by avoiding the 2-bolt belay and climbing up to the final two bolts. **Pitch 4:** Climb a short pitch up a right-leaning flake (5.0) to a ledge with a bolt anchor. Move the belay up and right around boulders to the base of a slab (gear anchor, 1 to 2 inches). Climb an easy (but unprotected) low-angle slab diagonally up and left to the top. 2-bolt belay/rappel anchor. **Descent:** Make a short rappel down to the big ledge (the finish of *Right On*), then rappel from another bolt anchor (100 feet) to the base. Scramble (3rd class) through boulders, staying well away from the cliff for the easiest descent back down to the base.

Saddle Rock—Northwest Face

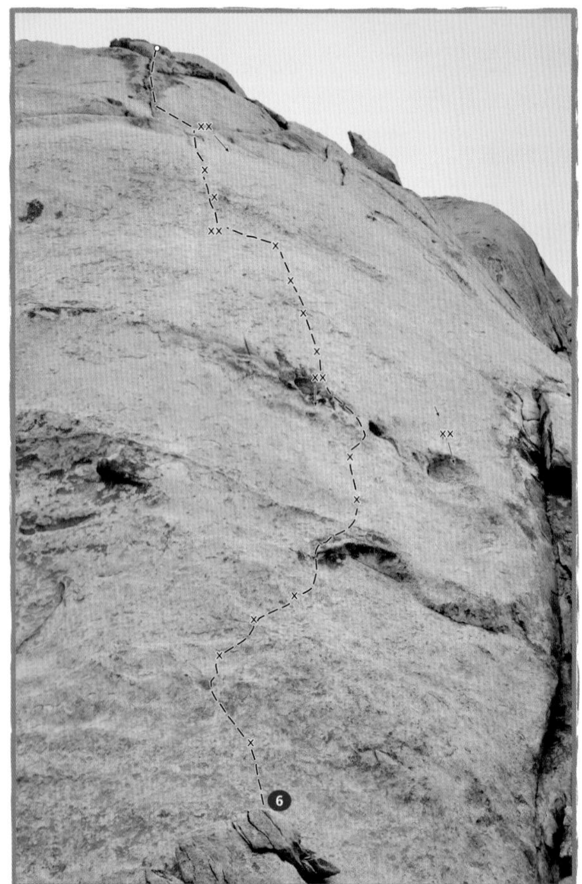

13. Jumbo Rocks

Conan's Corridor at Jumbo Rocks is approached by walking through a narrow chasm. It has a good number of trad crack climbs and a great sport climb on somewhat rough rock. The cliff is in the sun in the morning and the shade in the afternoon.

Getting there: From the Intersection Rock Junction, drive south on Park Boulevard (the road eventually curves east, then northeast) for 8.4 miles to its junction with the Jumbo Rocks Campground road (7.9 miles from the North Entrance). There is parking on both sides of Park Boulevard.

The approach starts at the Skull Rock Trailhead (GPS: N33° 59.531'/ W116° 04.105'), which is located on the north side of the road at the junction of Park Boulevard and the Jumbo Rocks Campground road. Walk east on the trail for about 350 yards to where it bends sharply to the left (north). Go another 200 feet and leave the Skull Rock Trail, turning left (west), and follow a trail just right of a large, flat slab of rock. Walk west through the canyon

Conan's Corridor

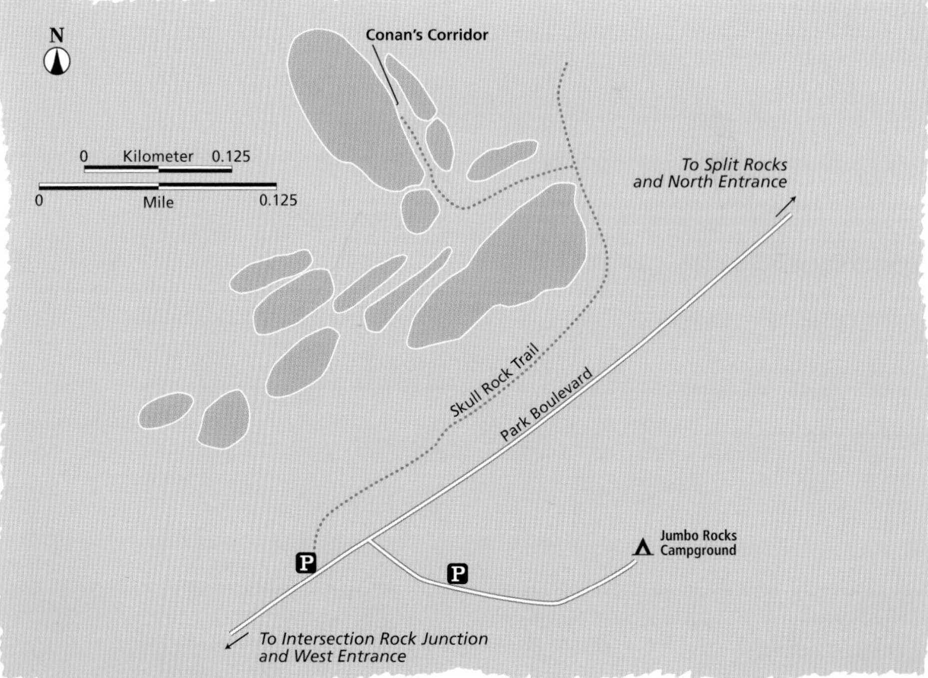

(with a bit of scrambling over boulders) for about 300 feet, then turn right (north) and enter the narrow Conan's Corridor. Once you walk through this chimney-like passage, the Corridor Cliff will be immediately to your left. Crag GPS: N33° 59.649' / W116° 03.974'

Descent: You can rappel 100 feet from the *Boulderado* anchor (very exposed to get to, so you may want a belay), or make a circuitous scramble off (3rd class) by heading left (south) from the top, then back down around through the "corridor" to the base. You can also descend off to the right (north), but this involves a bit of 5th-class downclimbing.

CONAN'S CORRIDOR

1. Spiderman (5.10b) Suprisingly sustained jamming up a long, vertical crack that widens at the top. Gear anchor. **Pro:** to 4 inches.

2. Colorado Crack (5.9) A popular crack climb with good pro. **Pro:** to 3 inches.

3. Boulderado (5.11a) Sport. Climb the face (5.9) up to a right-leaning seam with some stout lieback moves. 10 bolts to a 2-bolt lower-off anchor (100 feet).

4. Boulder Dice (5.10b) Clip the first three bolts on *Boulderado,* then traverse right and climb a vertical crack. **Pro:** to 3 inches; use slings on the bolts.

5. Gem (5.8) You might want to tape up for this one. This is a solid hand to fist jam crack with good pro and very coarse rock. **Pro:** to 3 inches.

Conan's Corridor

14. Split Rocks

The Split Rocks area offers a diverse array of cliffs and towers in a less crowded region of the Park. The area is known for its classic crack climbs on coarse rock.

Getting there: From the Intersection Rock Junction, drive south on Park Boulevard (the road eventually curves east, then northeast) for 9.7 miles and turn left onto the Split Rocks day-use area road. From the North Entrance, drive 6.6 miles and turn right. Drive 0.5 mile farther to the parking area, which has an outhouse (GPS: N34° 00.573' / W116° 03.356').

Split Rocks

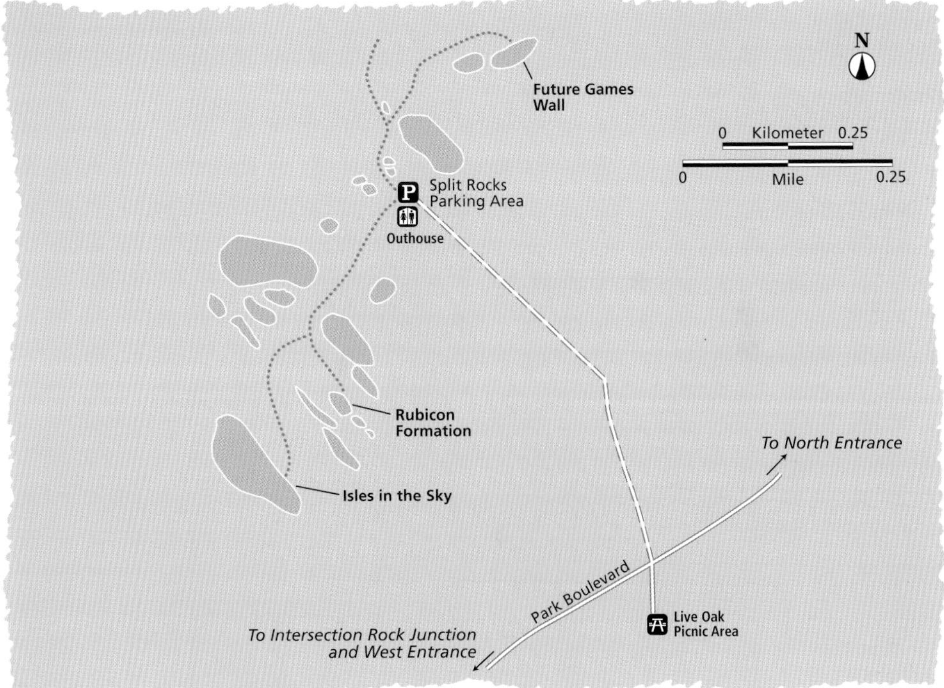

Rubicon Formation

RUBICON FORMATION

This beautiful tower has one of Joshua Tree's best 5.10 finger cracks. The climb is in the sun in the morning and the shade in the afternoon.

Finding the crag: From the parking area, walk southwest on a climber's trail for about 300 yards, passing a large rock formation on your left, then turn left and walk another 150 yards. The Rubicon formation will be on your right. Crag GPS: N34° 00.377' / W116° 03.433'

1. Rubicon (5.10c) Start on the right and climb a wide hand crack (3 inches), then traverse left to the main crack (optional belay here). Finger jams with nice edges for your feet take you to the top. Gear anchor. **Descent:** Rappel from bolts just to the right. **Pro:** to 3 inches, with extra .3 to .75 inches.

ISLES IN THE SKY

The highest formation in the Split Rocks area, Isles in the Sky is a striking formation with several excellent crack and face routes.

The cliff gets morning sun and afternoon shade.

Finding the crag: From the parking area, walk southwest on a climber's trail for about 500 yards, passing several large rock formations, then head left and walk another 300 yards. The Isles in the Sky formation will be on your right. The routes start above a large, flat ledge, accessed by a 4th- or easy 5th-class pitch. Crag GPS: N34° 00.325' / W116° 03.510'

Descent: Rappel from bolts just right of *Bird of Fire.*

Isles in the Sky

1. Dolphin (5.8) Climb the widening crack in the corner that ends in a strenuous off-width. Bring some big cams and don't underestimate this one. **Pro:** to 6 inches (#5 camalot or equivalent). On toprope, try stemming up the entire corner (5.10)!

2. Young Guns (5.11d or 5.10b) This is the 5-bolt face just left of *Bird of Fire* with the crux being the steep headwall at the top. You can traverse right to *Bird of Fire* after the third bolt for an easier (5.10b) route. **Pro:** a small to medium piece for the start.

3. Bird of Fire (5.10a) A tad runout to the first placement, but after that it's very well protected. Face climb up to, then finger jam the steepening crack to a hand-jamming finish. 2-bolt belay anchor. **Descent:** A 2-bolt rappel anchor is 10 feet to the right. **Pro:** to 3 inches.

John Long made the first ascent of *Bird of Fire* in 1974, and it is considered to be one of the best crack routes in Joshua Tree. Long recalls the first ascent: "I was hiking around with Ray Ochoa hunting for new routes. The area seemed very obscure at the time. The formation caught my eye. It looked almost regal or noble, perched up there like a king on a throne. Those were my haydays when I was climbing hard cracks and off-widths all the time. I free soloed *Dolphin* on sight, then we did *Bird of Fire*."

Jill Carpenter firing the stellar finger and hand crack *Bird of Fire* (5.10a), Isles in the Sky. PHOTO GREG EPPERSON

FUTURE GAMES WALL

This cliff has two great moderate crack climbs. It faces north and receives very little sun most of the year, so it's a good spot to find shade during warmer conditions.

Finding the crag: From the parking area, walk just left of the huge Split Rocks boulder that sits just north of the parking area. After about a hundred feet you'll see a climber's trail marker sign that reads FUTURE GAMES WALL. Thirty feet beyond the sign, veer right off the main trail and head through a gap in the boulders. After a few hundred feet of rough climber's trail, you'll come across more trail markers. Ten minutes of hiking time gets you to the crag. Crag GPS: N34° 00.708' / W116° 03.205'

Descent: An easy (2nd class) walk off the left (northeast) side.

1. Continuum (5.8+) Climb vertical thin cracks to a burly, right-slanting hand crack. **Pro:** to 3.5 inches.

2. Invisibility Lessons (5.9) Jam the steep finger to hand crack on the right side. **Pro:** to 3 inches.

Future Games Wall

Joshua Tree sunset.

15.

Indian Cove

Due to its lower elevation and sheltered, south-facing cliffs, Indian Cove is a good choice for cold winter days. With an elevation of around 3,200 feet, Indian Cove is 1,000 feet lower than the Hidden Valley area, making it a warmer choice when winter cold fronts, and their associated cruel winds, sweep through the area. The south facing cliffs can be too hot to comfortably climb during the warmer months.

Getting there: From the intersection of Highway 62 and Park Boulevard, drive east (toward Twentynine Palms) on Highway 62 (aka Twentynine Palms Highway) for 9 miles and turn right at Indian Cove Road. Drive 1 mile to the Indian Cove Ranger Station. There is no day-use fee for Indian Cove. Follow the directions below to the individual cliffs.

Indian Cove

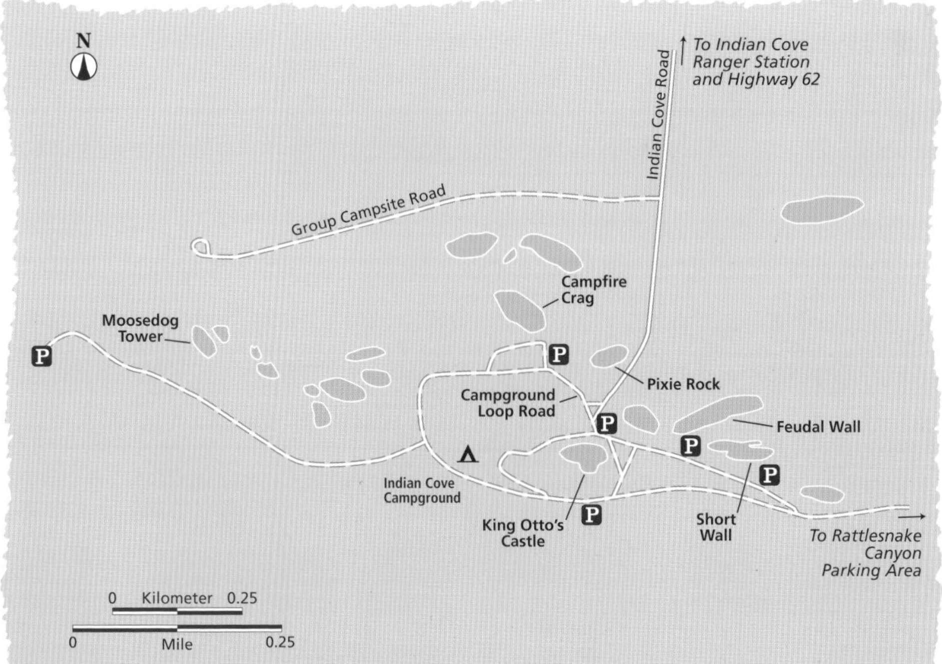

PIXIE ROCK

Pixie Rock's granite is very featured, offering excellent face climbing. The central slab is a great place to set up topropes for beginners. The crag faces south and is sheltered from north winds, so it's a good choice on cold winter days.

Finding the crag: From the ranger station, drive 1.8 miles to the campground loop road. Turn left and you'll see the day-use parking area immediately on your left. Pixie Rock is 100 yards to the north of the parking area. Crag GPS: N34° 05.545' / W116° 09.185'

Descent: Scramble (3rd class) off the opposite (north) side. You can also downclimb an easy 5th-class corner to the left of *Silent Scream.*

1. Lascivious Conduct (5.11c) Climb past three bolts over a tough bulge on the far left side. 2-bolt belay/rappel anchor.

2. Vaino's Lost in Pot (5.7 R/X) The face left of the center crack makes for a great toprope. Bolt anchor. **Pro:** A few cams from 2 to 4 inches are useful in rigging a toprope anchor.

3. Who's First (5.6 PG) Face climb 30 feet up to the central crack. Bolt anchor. **Pro:** A few cams from 2 to 3 inches are useful in rigging a toprope anchor.

4. Rhythm of the Heart (5.8 X) The face to the right of the center crack. No pro, but a great toprope. Bolt anchor. **Pro:** A few cams from 2 to 4 inches are useful in rigging a toprope anchor.

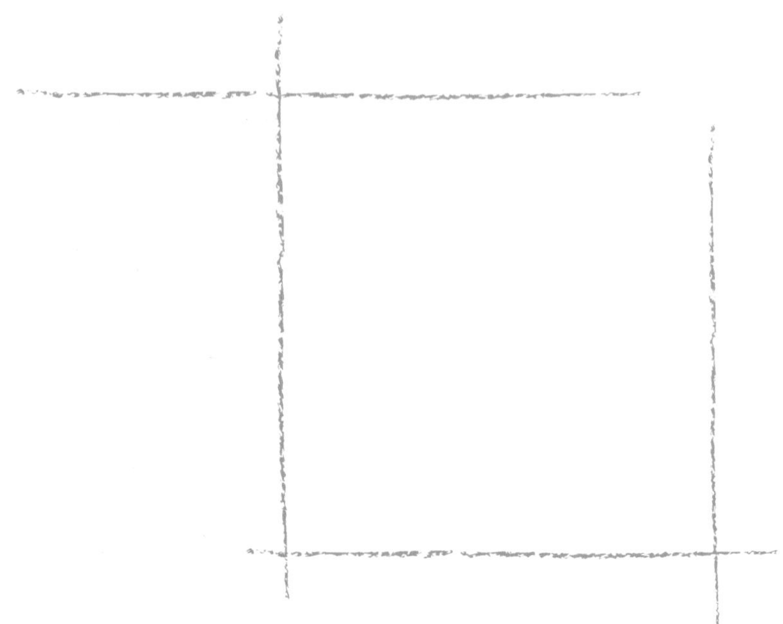

Pixie Rock

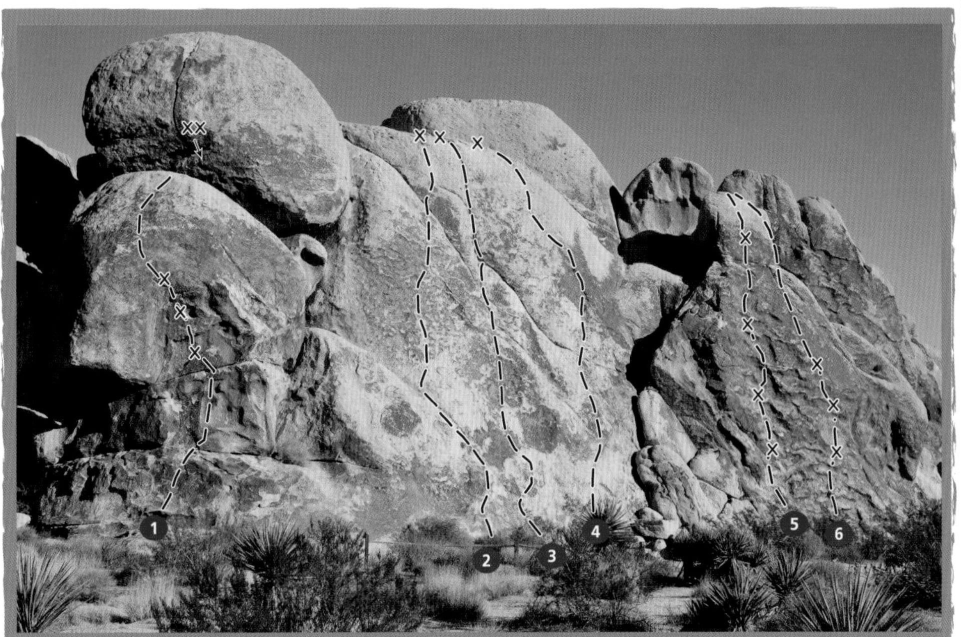

5. Silent Scream (5.10a) Climb the steep, juggy face past four bolts. Gear anchor (1.5 to 4 inches). **Pro:** A medium cam can be placed between the last two bolts.

6. Silent but Deadly (5.11b) Climb the challenging 3-bolt face just right of *Silent Scream*. Gear anchor (1.5 to 4 inches).

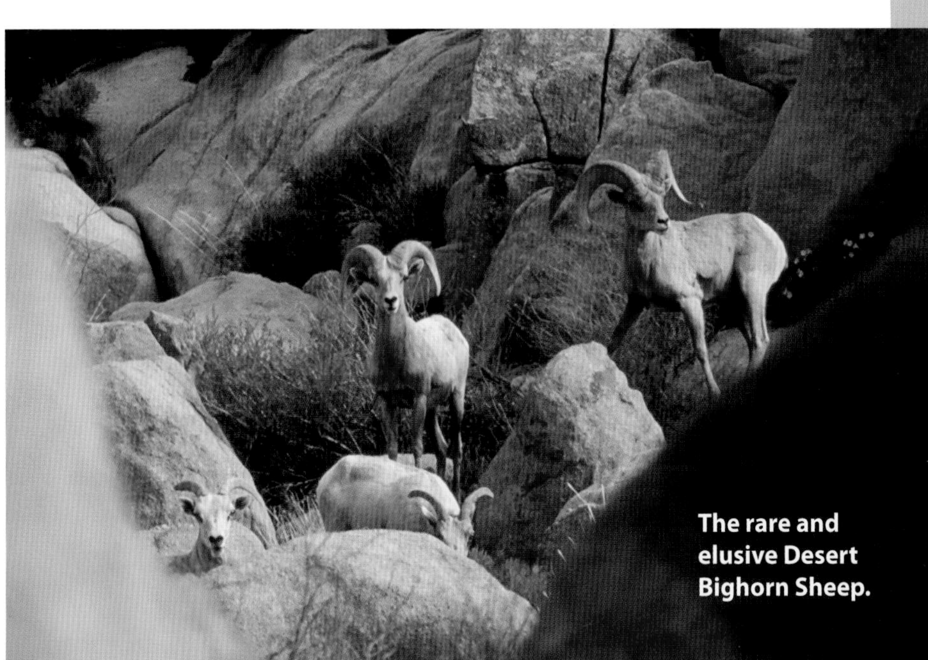

The rare and elusive Desert Bighorn Sheep.

Campfire Crag—North Face

CAMPFIRE CRAG

In contrast to all the south-facing walls in Indian Cove, this large cliff faces north and is shady most of the day—a good choice for warmer weather.

Finding the crag: From the ranger station, drive 1.8 miles to the campground loop road. Turn right and go 0.1 mile to a small parking area on the right, just before campsite 40 (GPS: N34° 05.679' / W116° 09.449'). Campfire Crag is the large formation just to the west. Walk around the right side of Campfire Crag (toward the campfire amphitheater), and the north face of Campfire Crag will be on your left. Crag GPS: N34° 05.745' / W116° 09.482'

1. Bonfire (5.11b) Climb an unprotected slab (5.0) to a very steep headwall with seven bolts. 2-bolt belay/rappel anchor (90 feet). **Pro:** A cam (2 to 4 inches) can be placed at the ledge below the first bolt.

Campfire Crag—North Face, Right Side

2. Presupposition (5.11d PG) Excellent climbing up thin seams on a steep, varnished wall. 2-bolt belay/rappel anchor on top (70 feet). **Pro:** thin to 2.5 inches.

3. Prejudicial Viewpoint (5.11b PG) Climb the right-leaning thin crack. Gear anchor. **Descent:** Rappel *Presupposition.* **Pro:** to 3 inches.

4. Campfire Girl (5.8 or 5.12a) Jam the well-protected finger crack (5.8) to a 2-bolt belay/rappel anchor. **Pro:** to 2 inches. The entire (rarely done) pitch continues above the anchor past three more bolts (5.12a) to a higher 2-bolt lower-off anchor (less than 100 feet).

> The first ascent of *Campfire Girl* was done as an aid climbing demonstration for a Girl Scout group. John Long toproped the first free ascent of the entire pitch in 1978, one of Joshua Tree's most difficult climbs at the time.

KING OTTO'S CASTLE

This tower faces south and is sheltered from north winds, making it a good choice for a cold winter's day. King Otto's Castle has some of the best face climbs in Indian Cove.

Finding the crag: From the ranger station, drive 1.8 miles to the campground loop road. Turn left and then take the next right, following the campground road to a small parking area on the left, just past campsite 29. King Otto's Castle is directly behind campsites 30 and 31. Crag GPS: N34° 05.523' / W116° 09.390'. **Occupied campsite rule:** If campers are in these sites, please ask their permission before climbing the routes.

Descent: There are several bolted rappel anchors on top (rappels are less than 100 feet).

1. Goodbye Mr. Bond (5.10c) Climb the steep face past four bolts to a 2-bolt anchor. **Pro:** a few 1.5- to 2.5-inch cams.

2. Casino Royale (5.11a PG) Start on *Sweat Band.* When your feet are just above the second bolt, traverse straight left past a bolt (5.10+) over to a seam. Make a tough move to gain the fourth bolt (5.11a), then follow the seam (5.10+) past easier face climbing and two more bolts to the top. 6 bolts to a 2-bolt belay/rappel anchor (90 feet).

3. Sweat Band (5.10b/c PG) Climb an easy but unprotected slab to a steeper headwall with six bolts. A couple of the bolts are in odd spots and awkward to clip. The climbing is a bit easier if you climb to the right of the bolts. 6 bolts to a 2-bolt belay/rappel anchor.

4. Tarawassi Wiggle (5.9 PG/R) Climb the start of *Plain But Good Hearted,* then climb the thin crack just left of *Leaving Las Vegas.* At the top the crack peters out. Runout (5.8 R) face climbing gets you to the top. **Pro:** a good selection of thin to medium nuts and cams to 1 inch.

5. Leaving Las Vegas (5.10b) Climb the start of *Plain But Good Hearted,* then climb directly up the face past five bolts to a 2-bolt anchor. **Pro:** to 1 inch for the start.

6. Plain But Good Hearted (5.6 PG) Climb a seam up to a crack in a corner. Near the top the crack ends—move left on exciting face moves up to the top. (You can also lower off the *Leaving Las Vegas* bolt anchor.) **Pro:** to 3.5 inches. Save a 1.5 inch cam (#1 camalot) for the top face.

King Otto's Castle

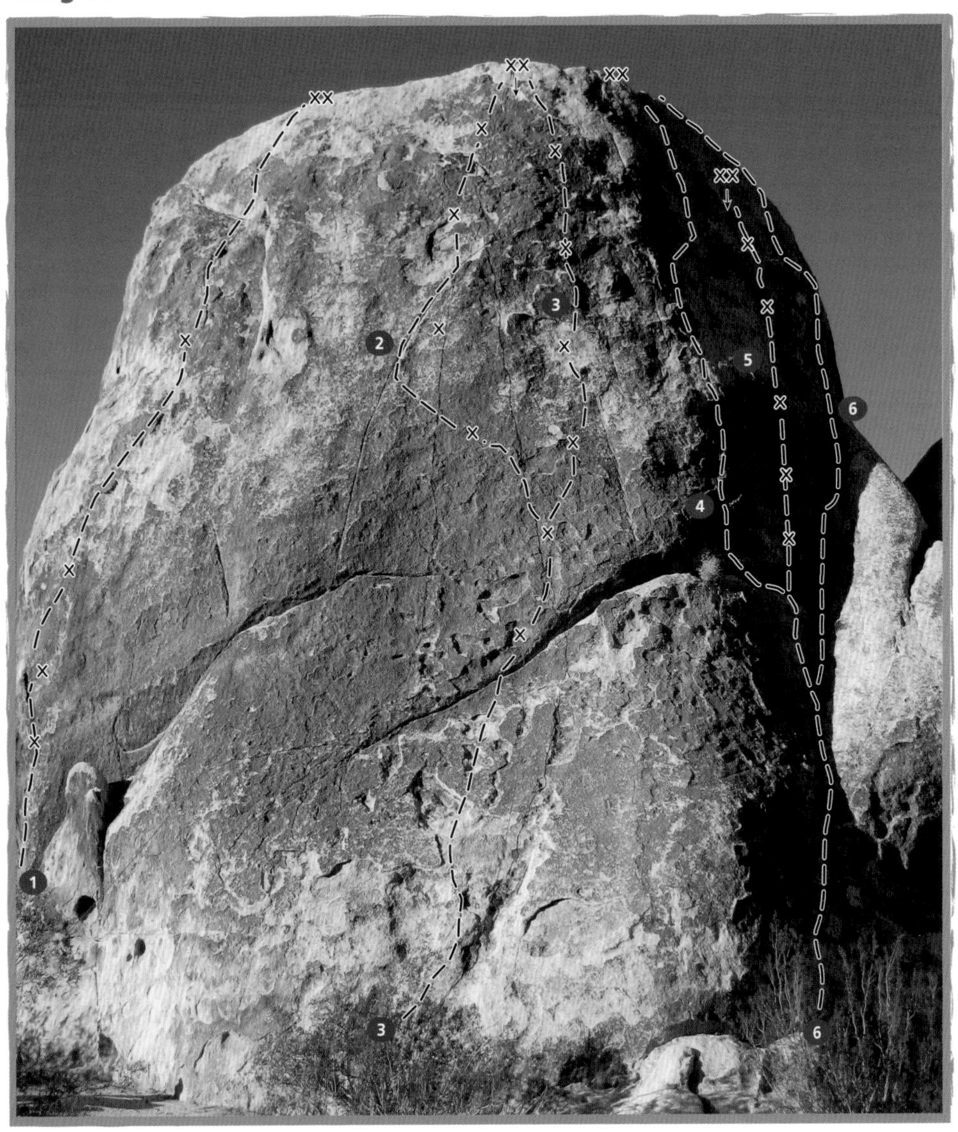

MOOSEDOG TOWER

This is the towering formation with a unique summit directly behind campsites 82 and 83 near the west end of Indian Cove Campground. The climbs face south and are in the sun most of the day. The summit is very exposed during windy conditions.

Finding the crag: From the ranger station, drive 1.8 miles to the campground loop road. Turn right and drive all the way to the west end of the campground road to a day-use parking area (GPS N34° 05.675' / W116° 10.114'). Walk back (east) down the campground road about 100 yards. Moosedog Tower is the large formation to the left, directly behind campsites 82 and 83. Crag GPS: N34° 05.663' / W116° 09.390'. **Occupied campsite rule:** If campers are in these sites, please ask their permission before climbing the routes.

Descent: Scramble across the summit ridge to the north side and make an overhanging rappel from bolts (less than 100 feet).

1. Third Time's a Charm (5.10b/c) Climb the classic left-leaning corner on the left side of the face in one long pitch (190 feet) or two pitches. The rock is poor at the start but quickly improves. The crux is protected by a bolt and is somewhat height-dependent. There is a belay stance about two-thirds up the route. **Pro:** to 3 inches.

2. Direct South Face (5.9) An Indian Cove classic. **Pitch 1:** Climb the left-facing dihedral up to the big roof, out the right side (crux), then up a fractured face to a belay in an alcove with a bolt. **Pitch 2:** Climb either a left-leaning crack on the left or the right-slanting crack on the right (both 5.8), then face climb up to a belay in a notch. **Pitch 3:** Climb a short face up to a crack that leads to the top. **Pro:** to 3 inches.

3. Tranquility (5.6 PG) A fun excursion. **Pitch 1:** Start from a block up and right from *Direct South Face* and climb an easy (5.3) face up to a ledge. **Pitch 2:** From the left end of the ledge, climb a very exposed arête (5.6) up to a belay in a notch. **Pitch 3:** Climb a short face (5.6) up to a crack that leads to the top. **Pro:** to 3 inches; include some slings to tie off flakes.

Moosedog Tower

Feudal Wall Overview

FEUDAL WALL

This large, multifaceted cliff faces south, making it a good choice for cold days. It is in the sun most of the day.

Finding the crag: From the ranger station, drive 1.8 miles to the campground loop road. Turn left and drive 0.1 mile to a day-use parking area on the left, just past campsite 7. Crag GPS: N34° 05.571' / W116° 09.890'

Feudal Wall

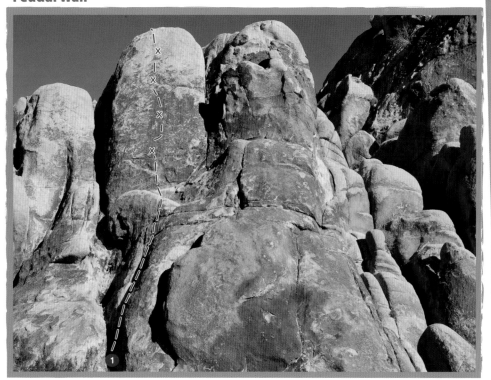

1. Coyote in the Bushes (5.10a) Climb a face past a flake, then smear up a slab with four bolts. **Descent:** Scramble (3rd class) off to the right, down a gully. **Pro:** 0.5- to 1-inch cams plus some large (1.5- to 4-inch) cams for the anchor.

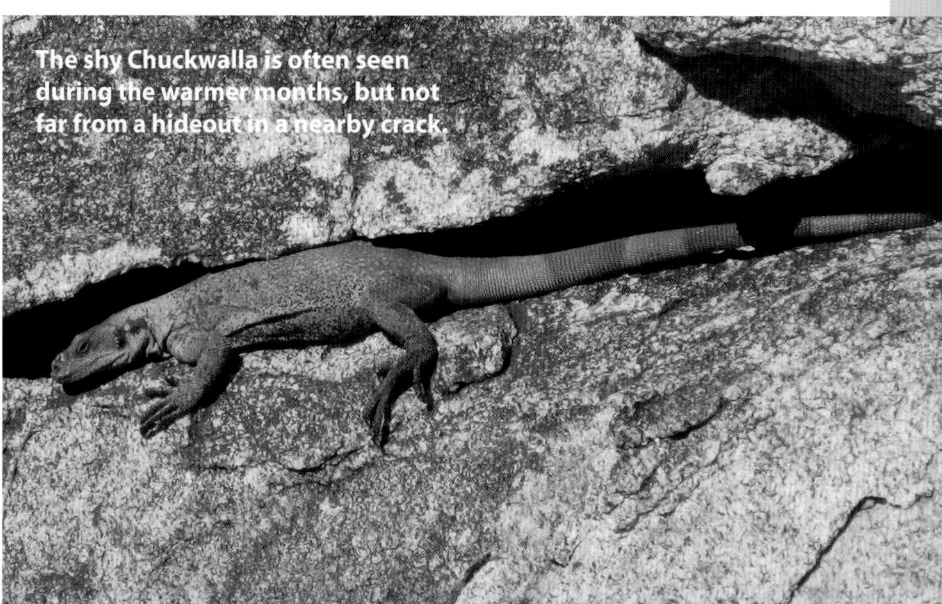

The shy Chuckwalla is often seen during the warmer months, but not far from a hideout in a nearby crack.

Feudal Wall

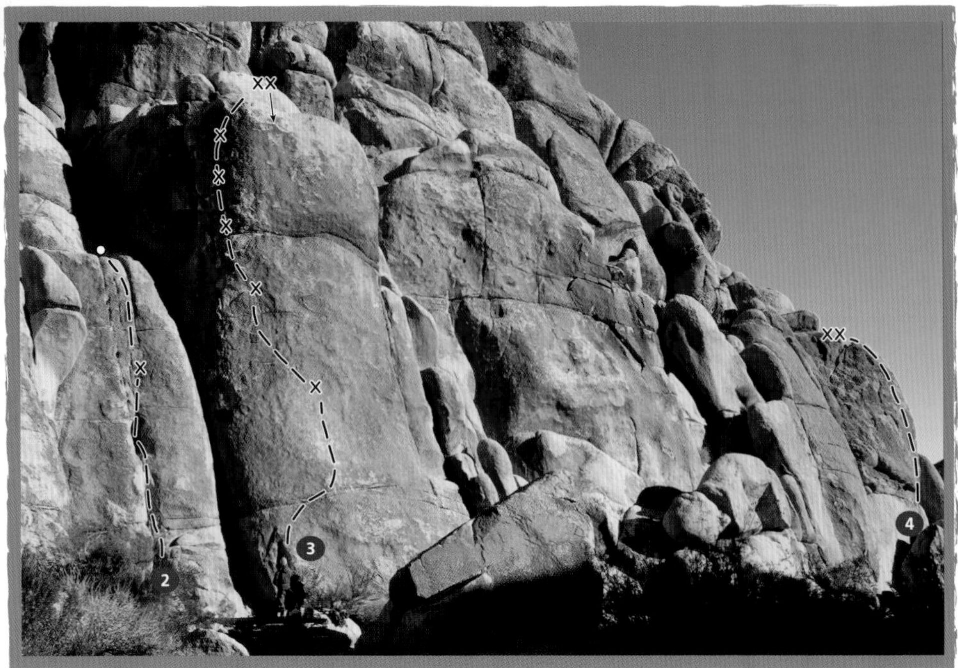

2. Duchess (5.6) **Pitch 1:** Fun face and crack climbing immediately behind the picnic table. Climb the pocketed crack past a bolt up to a ledge with a gear anchor. You can scramble off to the left after the first pitch, or climb up and right to the *Monaco* rap anchor. **Pitch 2:** The rarely done second pitch climbs an intimidating chimney with a difficult exit at the top, then moves right up cracks to the top. **Descent:** Downclimb (4th class) off the opposite (north) side of the formation. **Pro:** to 3 inches.

3. Monaco (5.11b/c) Climb the left side of the impressive buttress, starting with a steep slab to slightly overhanging face climbing that finishes with a very thin crux. 5 bolts to a 2-bolt belay/rappel anchor. The thin crack just to the right of *Monaco* is a fun toprope (*The Castrum,* 5.10a).

Feudal Wall

4. Pet or Meat (5.10d) Sport. Climb steep and tricky moves past four bolts to a 2-bolt belay/rappel anchor (less than 100 feet).

The route name *Pet or Meat* comes from the Michael Moore movie *Roger and Me.* A woman from Flint, Michigan, was so down on her luck that she raised and sold rabbits. She would skin some to sell as meat and sell the others as pets. Her advertisement read "Pet or Meat."

SHORT WALL

The climbs on this sunny, south-facing cliff aren't the best in Joshua Tree, but the crag has much to offer. You can park your car almost at its base. With over two dozen routes within a short distance, you can toprope, lead, or solo a bunch of routes in rapid succession. Some medium to large cams and a length of static rope are handy to rig topropes. This area bakes in the sun, so it's best during cooler conditions.

Getting there: From the ranger station, drive 1.8 miles to the campground loop road. Turn left and drive 0.2 mile to a day-use parking area on the left. The crag is just a few feet away! Crag GPS: N34° 05.545' / W116° 09.185'

Descent/access to the top: Walk around the right (east) side, then scramble up (3rd class) the back (north) side to access the top of the right side. To get up to and down from the left (west) side requires some serious scrambling (4th and 5th class)

Short Wall—Left Side

1. Step'n Out (5.10a/b PG) Climb a shallow thin crack. 2-bolt belay/rappel anchor. **Pro:** tiny cams (offset cams are handy) to 1.75 inches.

2. Double Trouble (5.10a TR) The face just right of *Step'n Out.*

Short Wall—Left Side

3. Mad Race (5.4) Jam the vertical crack. The downclimb off to the right is just about as difficult as the route!

4. Fluff Boy (5.8) Start on *Mad Race,* move right up a flake, then up the face past two bolts. 2-bolt anchor on top. **Pro:** to 3 inches.

5. Belay Girl (5.10d) Sustained, 4-bolt slab to a 2-bolt anchor.

6. Rif Raff Roof (5.10b) Start in a left-facing corner, then jam a crack over a small roof and continue to the top.

7. Bombay (5.8) Jam the vertical crack. **Pro:** to 3 inches.

8. Calcutta (5.8) Stem and jam the crack through a bulge. **Pro:** to 3 inches.

9. Left V Crack (5.11b R) A couple of bouldery moves. Usually toproped.

10. Right V Crack (5.10b/c) Maybe the best route at the Short Wall. Jam and lieback the right-slanting thin crack. Good pro, but strenuous to place. Greasy and harder on a hot day. **Pro:** to 2.5 inches.

11. Face to Face (5.11c TR) Climb the crimpy, thin face just right of the *Right V Crack,* passing a horizontal, then up a vertical seam.

12. Linda's Crack (5.6) Wide crack.

13. Linda's Face (5.6 R) No pro.

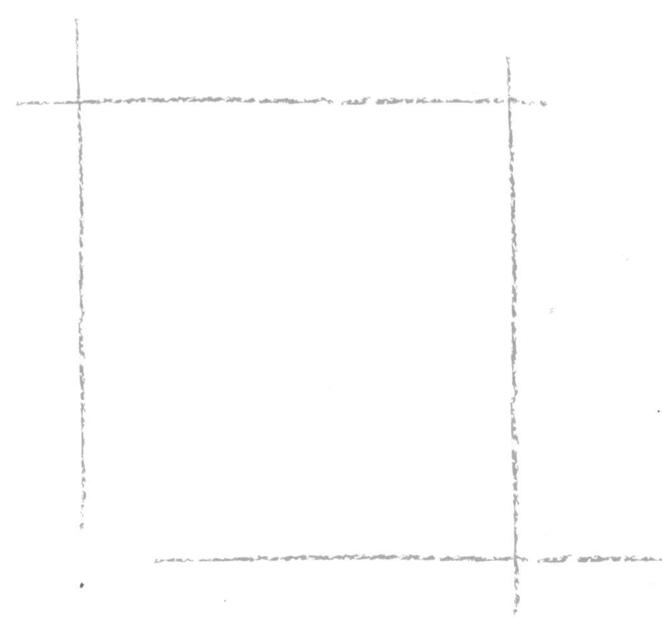

Short Wall—Right Side

1. Chockstone Chimney (4th class)

2. Tight Shoes (5.8 R) Thin hold slab climbing.

3. Double Crack (5.4) Hand crack.

4. Up To Heaven (5.8 R) Fun face climbing.

5. Toe Jam Express (5.4) Hand crack.

6. Steady Breeze (5.9 X) Unprotected face. The crux is at the bottom, then 5.7 to the top.

7. SOB (5.6) Hand crack.

8. Morning Warm Up (5.9 X) Unprotected face, crux near the start.

9. Afternoon Shakedown (5.11a X) Crux start to an easier face.

10. Gotcha Bush (5.6 X) Face climb, no pro.

11. Right N Up (5.8 X) Crack to unprotected face.

12. Donna T's Route (5.5) Short hand crack on far right side.

Short Wall—Right Side

Index

D

E

F

M

N

O

P

About the Author

Bob Gaines began rock climbing at Joshua Tree in the 1970s. Since then he has pioneered over 400 first ascents in the park. Bob began his career as a professional rock climbing guide in 1983 and is the owner of Vertical Adventures Rock Climbing School, which offers classes and guided climbs at Joshua Tree. In 2008 Vertical Adventures was voted the #1 rock climbing school in America by *Outside* magazine.

Bob has worked extensively in the film business as a climbing stunt coordinator. He has coordinated over thirty television commercials, and he was Sylvester Stallone's climbing instructor for the movie *Cliffhanger.* Bob doubled for William Shatner in the movie *Star Trek V,* as Capt. Kirk free-soloing on El Capitan in Yosemite.

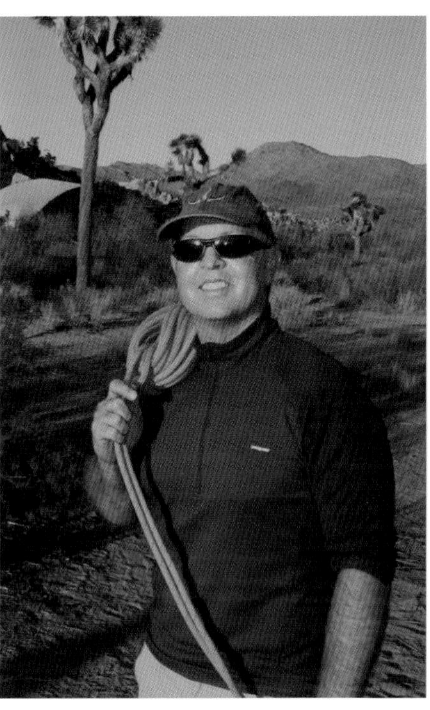

Bob is an AMGA Certified Rock Climbing Instructor and teaches the AMGA Single Pitch Instructor Course at Joshua Tree. He has worked extensively training U.S. military special forces, including U.S. Navy Seals, and is known for his technical expertise in anchoring and rescue techniques.

Bob is also the co-author of *Rock Climbing Tahquitz and Suicide Rocks* (with Randy Vogel) and *Climbing Anchors* (with John Long). Bob splits his time between his residences in Irvine and Joshua Tree, California.

What's So Special about Unspoiled, Natural Places?

Beauty Solitude Wildness Freedom Quiet Adventure
Serenity Inspiration Wonder Excitement
Relaxation Challenge

There's a lot to love about our treasured public lands, and the reasons are different for each of us. Whatever your reasons are, the national **Leave No Trace** education program will help you discover special outdoor places, enjoy them, and preserve them—today and for those who follow. By practicing and passing along these simple principles, you can help protect the special places you love from being loved to death.

The Principles of Leave No Trace

- Plan ahead and prepare
- Travel and camp on durable surfaces
- Dispose of waste properly
- Leave what you find
- Minimize campfire impacts
- Respect wildlife
- Be considerate of other visitors

Leave No Trace is a national nonprofit organization dedicated to teaching responsible outdoor recreation skills and ethics to everyone who enjoys spending time outdoors.

To learn more or to become a member, please visit us at www.LNT.org or call (800) 332-4100.

Leave No Trace, P.O. Box 997, Boulder, CO 80306

FALCONGUIDES Outfit Your Mind
Home
Series
Authors
About Us
Trails Powered by trails.com
advanced search
Subscribe to Email
Featured content:
Best Climbs Denver and Boulder. Over 200 of the Best Routes in the Area. (by Stewart M. Green, photo by Stewart M. Green) read more +
Find your outdoor adventure
Experience Moab's World-Class Climbing
Soul of Yosemite
Categories
Outdoor Life
Regional Interest
Special Interests
Travel
Falcon Video
watch Falcon videos
facebook
Try Kris Carr's 21-Day Juice Cleanse!
crazy sexy
The Advanced Cyclist's Training Manual
Fitness and Skills for Every Rider
Following up on FalconGuides' successful The Cyclist's Training Manual, this advanced edition addresses the same broad audience of cyclists while focusing more intently on the core functions of training, bike set-up, technique, and health. More experienced riders will meanwhile be informed and inspired to take their cycling to new levels of achievement. Whatever one's particular interest in the many different cycling disciplines, The Advanced Cyclist's Training Manual is packed with advice, training plans, and encouragement to help anyone become a fitter, faster,...
read more +
Share / Save
Hiking Grand Canyon National Park, 3rd
A Guide to the Best Hiking Adventures on the North and South Rims
Backpacker magazine's Backpacking Basics
Planning, Preparing, and Packing